Boys and Girls of Colonial Days

Carolyn Sherwin Bailey

Originally published as *Boys and Girls of Colonial Days*
Copyright © 1917 by A. Flanagan Company, Chicago

Copyright © 2002 Christian Liberty Press
First edition, 1990
2006 Printing

Printed by
Christian Liberty Press
502 West Euclid Avenue
Arlington Heights, Illinois 60004
www.christianlibertypress.com

Revised by Michael J. McHugh
Edited by Edward J. Shewan
Copyedited by Diane Olson
Design and layout by Christopher Kou at
imagineering studios, inc.

Illustrations by Vic Lockman,
Colorized by Timothy Kou

ISBN 978-1-930092-38-9
      1-930092-38-5

Printed in the United States of America

Contents

Preface

Many young people in America today have very little idea of what life was like during the colonial period. This reader is designed to provide youngsters with a better understanding of how the events and personalities of colonial America affected the lives of young people who lived during this time in history.

It is our hope that this book will help to give children a fuller appreciation for the spirit of determination that young people had during the colonial period to support the cause of liberty. Indeed, if liberty is to survive and prosper in our beloved land, the children of America will need to be properly trained to understand and value the blessings of freedom and liberty. It is impossible for the light of freedom to burn out as long as it shines brightly in the hearts of a nation's youth.

May God bless all those who read this little volume.

The Publishers
Arlington Heights, Illinois

Chapter 1
The Pink Tulip

Peering over the edge of the boat rail, Love strained her weary blue eyes for a glimpse of land. The sun was like a ball of soft gold light, peering dimly through the haze. Suddenly, like a heavenly place, the city appeared. There were tall, shining towers, gold church spires, pointed roofs with wide red chimneys where the storks stood in one-legged fashion, and great windmills with their long arms stretched out to catch the four winds. The boat was soon to reach the city of Amsterdam, in the country of Holland. The boat was full of people who were looking for a place to live where they could worship God freely. These people were known as the Pilgrims.

Love Bradford, ten years old, flaxen haired, and as pretty as an English rose in June, wrapped her long, gray coat more closely around her and turned to one of the women on board.

"Do you think that my father may have taken another boat that sailed faster than this and is waiting for me on the shore, Mistress Brewster? The last words he said to me when he left me on the ship were 'Wait patiently until I come, Love; I will not be long.' That was many days ago."

Mistress Brewster turned away so the little girl might not see the tears that filled her eyes. Love's father, just before the ship that carried the Pilgrims from England had sailed, had been cast into prison by the king, because of his faith in Jesus Christ. Love was all alone, but Mistress Brewster did not want her to know that her father, Goodman Bradford, was imprisoned.

"Maybe your father will meet you some day soon in Holland. Surely, if he said that he would not be long, he will keep his word. See, Love, see the little boy down there in the fishing boat."

Love looked in the direction in which the woman pointed. A plump, rosy little boy with eyes as blue as Love's own and dressed in full brown trousers and clumsy wooden shoes sat on a big net in one end of the boat. He looked up as the sails of the little fishing craft glided closely alongside the boat that carried the wanderers from England. At first, he dropped his eyes in shyness at the sight of the little girl. Then he lifted them again and as his eyes met hers, the two children smiled at each other. It was like a flash of sunshine piercing the gray haze that hung over the sea.

There were friends waiting on the shore for every passenger except Love. These were older brothers, fathers, and other relatives who had made the pilgrimage from England a few months before and had homes ready for their family members. They climbed a long hill, very flat on the top, and reached by a flight of steps. Then they were as high as the trees that lined the beach and could look over the narrow streets, the tidy cottages with their red roofs, and the pretty gardens. There were many little canals, like blue ribbons, cutting through the green fields. Love walked into town with Mistress Brewster.

A Dutch housewife, dressed in a white cap and apron, met them and said, "Welcome to Amsterdam!" She put her hand on Love's yellow hair. "And in which house are you going to live, little English blossom?" she asked kindly.

Love looked up wonderingly into her face and there was a whispered consultation between Mistress Brewster and the Amsterdam woman. "Poor little blossom! She shall come home with me. There is always room for one more in the stork's nest," the Dutch woman said kindly. She took Love's hand and led her away from the others, and along the canal.

The house where they stopped was really very odd. It was made of red and yellow bricks and it stood on long posts sunk deep into the ground. The white kitchen door was so clean that it was hard to tell that they were walking into the kitchen. What a kitchen it was, so cozy and so quaint! The floor was made of white tiles and there was a charming little fireplace. It looked like a big brass pan filled with coals, and there was a shining copper kettle hung over it by a chain from the ceiling. The kettle bubbled and sang a cheerful welcome to Love. There were stiff white curtains at the windows, and on the sill of one window was a row of blossoming plants. Blue and white dishes and a pair of tall candlesticks stood on a shelf. Love could see a bright sitting room beyond and another room where there was a strange bed, built on the wall and stretching almost from the floor to the ceiling.

"Jan, Jan," the woman called. "Come in from the garden and offer your new little English sister a seed cake. You may have one yourself, too. You have often wished for a playmate and here one has come to live in the house with you."

The door opened slowly and in came Jan. He did not look up at first. Then his eyes caught Love's. It was the little boy from the fishing boat. It was his dear mother who had offered to take care of lonely little Love.

"You may help me drive the dogs that draw the milk wagon," Jan said to Love the next morning, after they had become well acquainted over their breakfast of milk and oatmeal cakes.

"And so I can help to earn money for your kind mother," Love said with shining eyes.

Jan had two dogs and a little two-wheeled cart to which he harnessed them every morning. Into the cart

his mother put two shining pails of milk and a long-handled dipper for measuring. Today she also put in some round, white cheeses and golden balls of butter. Off started the cart along the narrow street with Love running along one side and Jan clattering along in his wooden shoes on the other side. The dogs knew where to stop almost as well as Jan did, for they had made the trip quite often. The cheese and butter were soon gone, and everyone had a pleasant smile for the little English girl. At one cottage, a Dutch housewife brought out a strange, earth-colored bulb that she put in Love's hands. Then, smiling down into the little girl's wondering face, she said:

"It is truly a rare one. I give it to you that you may plant it and tend it all winter. When the spring comes, you will have a finer one than any child in all Amsterdam."

Love thanked the woman, but she puzzled over the hard, dry bulb as she and Jan walked home beside the empty milk cart. "It looks like nothing but an onion. What good is it, Jan?"

Jan's eyes twinkled. "I know, but I won't tell," he said. "I want you to be surprised next spring. Come, Love, we will plant it in the corner of the garden that the sun shines on first in the spring. Then we will wait to see what grows."

As Jan dug a hole and Love planted the bulb, his words repeated themselves in the little girl's lonely heart. She remembered, too, what her dear father had said last to her, "Wait patiently until I come, Love." Would her patience bring her missing father back, Love wondered sorrowfully.

The days passed, with blue skies and the bright sun shining down upon the canal, and then grew shorter. The storks flew south, and Love was very happy. Her days with Jan were busy, merry ones. She, too, had wooden shoes now; and Jan's mother had made her a warm red skirt and velvet girdle and a green quilted coat. Love looked like a real little Dutch girl as she skated to school, with her knitting in her school bag to busy her fingers with when it was recess time.

There was never any place in England, Love thought, so merry as the frozen canal in front of her new home in Holland. Everybody was on skates; the market women with wooden yokes over their shoulders, from which hung baskets of vegetables; and even a mother skating and holding her baby in a snug nest made of a shawl on her back. The old doctor skated, with his pill bag on one arm, to see a sick patient at the other end of the town; and long rows of happy children glided by, holding each other's coats and twisting and twining about like a funny ribbon.

"Are you not glad, Love, that you came here to Holland to be my sister?" Jan asked as, holding her hand in his, he skated with Love to school.

"I am glad, Jan," Love warmly replied. "I feel as though it were a story book that I am living in, and you and your dear mother and our house and the canal were the pictures in it. But, oh, Jan, I wish very much that I could see my father—so tall and brave and strong!" Then she stopped. "We must be moving on, Jan," she said, "or we shall be late for school." But to herself, Love was saying, "Be patient."

Spring came early that year in Amsterdam. The ice melted and the canals were again blue ribbons of water. The sails of the windmills whirred, and the housewives scrubbed their sidewalks until the stones were clean enough to eat from. The storks built their nests in the red chimneys again, and everywhere the tulips burst into bloom. Love had never seen such beautiful flowers in all her life. There was no garden in Amsterdam so small or so poor as not to have a bed of bright red and yellow tulips.

With the first sunshine, Love went out to the garden where she and Jan had planted the ugly, hard bulb. How wonderful; her patience had been rewarded! There were two tall, straight green leaves and between

them—like a wonderful cup upon its green stem—a great, beautiful tulip. It was larger than any of the others. It was not red or yellow like the others, but pink, like a rose, or a sunrise cloud, or a baby's cheek.

"Jan! Mother! Come and see my tulip," cried Love, and then the three stood around the pink tulip in admiration.

"It is the most beautiful tulip in Amsterdam," said Jan.

"It is worth money," said his mother. "Someone would pay a good price for the bulb."

Love remembered what Jan's mother said. As the days passed and the pink tulip opened wider and showed a deeper tint each day, a plan began to form in the little girl's mind. She knew there was not very much money in Jan's home into which she had been so kindly welcomed. She knew, too, that nothing was so dear to the people of Holland as their tulips. Strange tales were told of how they sold houses, cattle, land—everything—to buy tulip bulbs.

One Saturday when Jan was away doing an errand for his mother, Love dug up her precious pink tulip and planted it carefully in a large flowerpot. With the pot hugged close to her heart, she went swiftly away from the house, down the long steps to the road that led along the coast of the sea below the dike. Here, where great merchant ships from all over the world anchored almost every day, Love felt sure that someone would see her tulip and want to buy it.

There was such a crowd—people of many nations busy unloading cargoes—that at first no one saw the little girl with the flower in her arms. Up and down the shore she walked, a little frightened but brave. She held the flower high, and called in her sweet voice, "A rare pink tulip. Who will buy my pink tulip?"

Intent on holding the flower carefully, she came suddenly in front of a man who had been walking in lonely fashion up and down the shore. She heard him call her name eagerly.

"Love! Love! Oh, my little Love!"

Looking up, Love almost dropped the tulip in her joy. Then she set it down and rushed into his arms.

"Father, dear Father! Oh, where have you been so long?" she cried.

It was a story told between laughter and tears. Goodman Bradford, only a short time since released from prison, had come straight to Amsterdam, but he had been able to find no trace of Love. Mistress Brewster had gone on with the Pilgrims to America, and there was no one to tell Goodman Bradford where his little daughter was. Now he could make a home for her and reward Jan's mother.

"I was patient," Love said, "as you told me to be, and see," she cried as, hand in hand, they reached the quaint little cottage where Jan and his mother stood at the door to greet them, "in good time they both came to me—the pink tulip and my father."

Comprehension Questions

1. What was the name of Love Bradford's father?

2. What country is well known for its tulip gardens?

3. How did Love Bradford try to make money?

4. Why was Love's father placed in prison in England?

5. How was Love Bradford's patience rewarded?

Chapter 2

Big Hawk's Decoration

See to it, Percival, that you win a colored ribbon from the schoolmaster today," Mistress Edwards said as she turned from her task of polishing the pewter platter to look at the boy who stood in the doorway of the log cabin.

"This is the day, I hear, on which the good-conduct ribbons are given out for the month, brightly dyed ones for the boys and girls whose lessons have been well learned, and black for the lazy students. There is no chance of your coming home to me tonight without a ribbon of merit, is there?" The colonial mother crossed the room and put her hands on her lad's shoulder, looking anxiously into his honest brown eyes.

"No, Mother," Percival answered. "At least I have hopes of winning a ribbon. Not once this month have I failed in my arithmetic, and I can read my chapters in the Bible as well as any child in school."

"That is good!" Mistress Edwards said, pulling the boy's long, dark coat more closely around him and smoothing the top of his tall hat.

Percival Edwards was a Puritan boy who lived many years ago, when America was young. The cabin that he was leaving to walk two miles across the clearing and through the woods to school was but a simple log home. A few straight chairs and a sturdy table made of logs stood by the fireplace. Several pewter utensils and a spinning wheel were almost the only furnishings in the living room. In one corner stood an old musket. Mistress Edwards looked toward it and remembered the past and the Indian wars.

"Will you come home as soon as school is out, Percival? I pray you do not linger on the way to play with the other boys and girls of the village. Remember, my boy, that your father is away with the horse these two days to bring back a piece of linsey-woolsey cloth and some flour from Boston for me. He is unlikely to come home for some days yet, and I am afraid at what I saw in the cornfield this morning."

"What did you see, Mother?" Percival's eyes opened wide with wonder.

"It was not so much what I saw, but what it may mean for us in the future," Mistress Edwards said. "It was only a flash of color, like painted feathers, among the withered stalks of corn. It reminded me of Big Hawk's headdress. If he were to find out that we were alone, one helpless woman and a boy of twelve here, I think it would go badly with us."

Percival laughed bravely. Then he reached up to kiss his mother good-bye.

"It was no more than a red-winged blackbird that you saw," he said, "or maybe it was a bright tanager. The birds are getting ready to flock now, for they feel the autumn chill in the air. But I will hurry home—with my ribbon."

Then he ran down the little path to the gate in the fence that surrounded the cabin, his speller under his arm, and his highheeled, buckled shoes making the dry leaves scatter as he went.

It was a long and lonely road to the log schoolhouse. Percival ran his way through the cornfield where the dried stalks, rattling in the cold wind, made him think of the songs that he had heard Big Hawk and his tribe sing the last time they had attacked the little colonial settlement. That had been some months ago now, and

Percival could find no traces of footprints or any other marks of Indians in the cornfield.

"My mother had a fear for nothing," Percival said to himself. He went through a bit of woods and pulled a small square of bark from one of the many birch trees that stood there, so white and still. It was for Percival to practice writing his lessons upon in school, and as he hurried on he repeated his multiplication tables over and over to be sure that he knew them well.

There were log cabins scattered here and there, and from these came other boys and girls who followed Percival to school. Deliverance Baxter joined Percival. She wore a long, thin brown frock, and her yellow hair was tucked tightly inside a close, white cap. A scarf was folded neatly around her neck, and she also wore big

buckles on her black shoes. Her eyes twinkled brightly as she talked to Percival.

"There is no doubt, Percival, that you will wear home the long streamers of red ribbon on your coat this afternoon. I have been quite as perfect as you in my lessons for the month, but woe is me, I did a great wrong yesterday. You know that Master Biddle, our schoolmaster, has just purchased a new wig from Boston town. The strands hair in the back were so unusually long and tied with such a large bow that they caught my eye when I was getting the pile of books from behind his desk. I know not, Percival, what mischief was in my fingers, but I tied Master Biddle's wig to his chair. When he stood up, why, the wig was almost pulled from his head; and I was forced to stay after school until dusk, sitting on the dunce's stool. I am very sorry that I was so foolish. As you can see, I have ruined my chance of receiving a ribbon now, Percival."

The boy laughed as he took the little girl's hand comfortingly in his. Reaching in his lunch bag, he took out a red apple and slipped it into the big sack that hung at her side.

"You were always a bit silly despite your Puritan dress and sober living, Deliverance," he said. "Never mind about the ribbon. If I should win it, why, there is all the more chance of its being yours the next time. Here we are! See to it, Deliverance, that you tie no more wigs today.... Oh, see how finely Master Biddle is dressed for giving out the prizes!" Percival said as they reached the schoolhouse door and took their places behind the rude desks, built of boards and resting on pegs in the floor.

Other children were quietly taking their places in the little schoolroom, the smaller ones perched on hard benches made of logs. They all looked in awe at the schoolmaster, who stood on a platform, facing them. He wore a nice velvet coat with long tails, and under it could be seen a very long waistcoat and a fine white shirt with stiffly-starched ruffles. His knee breeches were of velvet like his coat, and there were silver buckles at the knees as well as on his shoes. A stiffly-ironed collar was worn around his neck to keep his head straight as became the dignity of the times. Above all was his white powdered wig, neatly tied in the back.

Looking at Master Biddle alone was enough to make the children of the Colonies sit up very straight and recite their lessons as well as they could. There was a prayer first, and then the boys and girls recited their reading, spelling, and arithmetic. Their pencils were thick pieces of lead and their copy books were made of crude paper, sewn in the shape of books and carefully ruled by hand. At eleven o'clock came recess, and at the end of the afternoon came the awarding of the good-conduct ribbons.

"For perfect conduct," Master Biddle announced as he pinned a bow of blue ribbon to one boy's cape.

"For poor lessons!" he said, sadly, as he fastened a black bow to another. Then he held up a red bow with especially long, streaming ends.

"For perfect conduct, and for perfect lessons," he said, as he fastened the red ribbon bow to Percival Edwards's coat.

Today it would seem but a small prize, but in the eyes of these Puritan boys and girls of so many years ago, the bow of ribbon, its streamers of red gaily flying over the long cape of a boy or the dull linsey-woolsey frock of a little girl, was truly a mark of great honor. Ribbons were scarce and high in price in those days. Colors for children were almost forbidden, and for their elders as well. So Percival walked out of the school door at the end of the day with his head very high and started home as proudly as any soldier wearing a decoration for bravery.

He did not notice how the dusk was settling down all around him. The trees on either side made dark shadows and there was no sound except the flap of a partridge's wing or the rattle of a falling nut. He did not hear the soft footsteps behind him until Deliverance, breathless and her face white with fear, was upon him. She laid a soft hand on his shoulder and whispered in his ear:

"I beg you, Percival, to let me walk with you. I know that it is not far to my cabin, but all the way through these woods I have heard strange sounds and I believe, even now, that I see shapes behind the trees and bushes."

Percival took the timid little girl's hand and tried to laugh away her fears.

"So was my mother afraid this morning, at nothing," he said. "She was of a mind that she saw Indians—Oh!" The boy's voice was suddenly hushed.

Stepping out from his hiding place in full view of the children, like a great forest tree dressed in its gorgeous cloak of bright autumn leaves, stood the Indian chief,

Big Hawk. He wore his war paint and his festival head-dress of hawks' feathers. Slung over his clothes were his bow and a quiver full of new arrows. It seemed little more than a second before the edges of the path and the deep places among the trees on either side were alive with the Indians of Big Hawk's tribe.

Big Hawk looked at the frightened children, showing with gestures what was his plan. He pushed back the white cap from Deliverance's pale forehead and laid his hand on the girl's sunny hair. Then he pointed toward his tribe's camping place in the west. He wanted to take Deliverance there and hold her for a ransom. To Percival, he made gestures showing that he wished him to lead the way to the Edwards's cabin that he might plunder it before going back that night.

Deliverance clung, crying, to Percival. He tried to be brave, but it was a test for a man's courage, and he was only a boy.

It was a second's thought and a strange decision of a proud Indian that saved the two. The autumn wind, blowing through the trees, caught the ends of Percival's ribbon of honor and sent them, fluttering like tongues of flame, against the dark of the tree trunks. The bright color caught Big Hawk's eye, and he touched the bow on Percival's cloak with one hand.

Quick as a flash, a thought came to Percival. He drew back from Big Hawk's touch and put his own hands over the ribbon as if to guard it.

"Heap big chief!" Percival's voice rang out, brave and clear. Then, after waiting a second, he unpinned the red bow and held it high before Big Hawk's face.

"Big Hawk, heap bigger chief!" he said, as he went boldly up to the Indian and fastened the ribbon on his clothes. Then he motioned to Big Hawk to return to his camp and show the rest of the tribe his new decoration. A slow smile overspread Big Hawk's painted face. Then he turned and, motioning to his braves to follow him, went silently back through the woods, leaving Percival and Deliverance alone and safe.

Deliverance was the first to speak.

"My heart does beat so fast I can hardly breathe, Percival. Oh, but you are a brave boy! What shall we do now?" she asked.

"Run!" said Percival, without a moment's hesitation. "We had best run like rabbits, Deliverance!"

Hand in hand, the two scampered along, Percival helping the little girl over the rough places, until the light from a candle in Deliverance's cabin was in sight. Her father had come home early, and when the children told him of their adventure, he set out to warn the rest of the settlers of the danger so bravely averted and put them on guard against the Indians.

Percival went on home. His mother stood in the cabin door, anxious because he was so late.

"No ribbon? Oh, my lad, why have you disappointed me?" she said when she saw him.

"Big Hawk wears my decoration," Percival said, as he told his story. "But I think that Master Biddle would have rather had little Mistress Deliverance get his red bow," he finished, laughing.

Chapter 3

The Soap Making of Remember Biddle

"Do you think that you will be able to return by Thanks-giving Day?" Remember Biddle asked with almost a sob in her voice.

A little Puritan girl of long ago was Remember, dressed in a long, greenish-blue frock, heavy hobnailed shoes and wearing a blue scarf around her neck. She stood in the door of the little log farmhouse that looked out upon a dreary stretch of the Atlantic coast. The town of Plymouth Rock raised its gray head not so very far away.

No wonder Remember felt unhappy. Her mother was at the door, mounted upon their horse, and ready to leave for quite a long journey, as journeys were counted in those days. She was going with a bundle of herbs to care for a sick neighbor who lived a distance of ten miles away. It had been an urgent summons, brought by the mail carrier that morning. The neighbor was ill, indeed, and the fame of Mistress Biddle's herb brewing was well-known throughout the countryside.

22

She leaned down from the saddle to touch Remember's dark hair. The little girl had run out beside the horse and laid her cheek against his soft side. Her father was far away in Boston, attending to some important matters of business. Her mother's trip left Remember all alone. She repeated her question, "Shall I be alone for Thanksgiving Day, Mother, dear?"

Her mother turned away so that the little daughter might not see that her eyes were full of sorrow.

"I don't know, Remember. I sent a letter this morning by the mail carrier to Boston telling your father that I would wait for him at Neighbor Allison's, and if I could leave the poor woman, he could come home with me. I hope that we shall return in time for Thanksgiving Day; but if it should happen that you must be alone, take no thought of your loneliness. Think only of how much cause we have for being thankful in this free, fertile land of New England. And keep busy, dear child. You will find plenty to do in the house until my return."

Throwing the girl a good-bye kiss, Mistress Biddle gave the horse a light touch with her riding whip and was off down the road, her long, dark cloak blowing like a gray cloud on the horizon in the chilly November wind.

For a few moments, Remember leaned against the beams of the door listening to the call of a flock of flying crows and the crackling of the dried cornstalks in the field behind the house. Beyond the cornfield lay the brown and green woods, uncut, except by an occasional winding Indian trail. The neighboring cabins were so far away that they looked liked toy houses set on the edge of other fields of dried cornstalks. Looking again toward the woods, Remember shivered a little. She saw in imagination a tall, dark figure in bright blanket and trailing feather headdress walk out from the depths of the thicket of pines and oaks. Then she laughed.

"An Indian has not passed here since early in the summer," she said to herself. "Mother would not have left me here alone if she had not known that I would be safe. I will go in now and play that I am the mistress of this house, and I am getting it ready for company on Thanksgiving Day. It will be so much fun that I shall forget all about being a lonely little girl.

It was a happy time of play. Remember tied one of her mother's long aprons over her dress to keep it clean and began her busy work of cleaning the house and making it shine from cellar to ceiling. She sorted the piles of ruddy apples, winter squashes, and pumpkins in the cellar and rehung the slabs of rich bacon and the strings of onions. As she touched the bundles of savory herbs that hung near the cellar walls, Remember gave a little sigh.

"I see no chance of these being used in the stuffing of a fat turkey for Thanksgiving," she said to herself. "It may be that I shall have to eat nothing but mush and applesauce for my dinner, and all alone. Ah, what a day!" She began to sing in her sweet, child voice one of the hymns that she had learned at the big white meeting-house:

"The Lord is both my health and light; Shall men make me dismayed? Since God doth give me strength and might, Why should I be afraid?"

As she sang, Remember lifted a bucket of soft soap that stood on the cellar floor and dragged it up to the kitchen. Then she went to work with a willing hand.

Several days passed before Remember had cleaned the house to her satisfaction. On her hands and knees she scoured the floors, her rosy hands and arms drenched with the foaming soapsuds. Afterward, she sprinkled sand upon the spotless boards in pretty patterns as was the fashion in those days. She swept the brick hearth with a broom made of twigs, and she scoured the pewter and copper utensils until they were as bright as so many mirrors. She washed the wooden chairs until the bunch of cherries painted upon the back of each looked bright enough to pick and eat. She dusted the straight rush-bottomed chairs and the kettle that stood by the side of the fireplace. Even the tall clock in the corner had its round glass face washed. Then Remember stood in the center of the kitchen looking at the good result of her work.

"My mother, herself, could have done no better!" she thought. Then she looked at the keg that had held their precious store of soft soap. There was no soap to be bought in those long-ago days; the Puritans needed to make their own soap because there were no super-markets.

"I have used up all the soap! Oh, what will my mother say at such waste? What shall I do?" Remember said in dismay.

She sat down by the fire and thought. Suddenly, she jumped up. A happy plan came to her mind.

"I will make some soap," Remember said to herself. "I have helped Mother make soap often and I should try to make some now. It is several days until Thanksgiving and I am sadly idle with nothing to do, now that the house is put so well in order."

The soap-making barrel, a hole bored in the bottom, stood in a corner of the cellar; it was light enough that

Remember could easily handle it, for she was strong for her twelve summers and winters. In the bottom of the barrel she put a layer of clean, fresh straw from the shed and over this she filled the barrel as far as she could with wood ashes. Then she rolled and tugged and lifted the barrel to a bench that stood by the kitchen door, taking care that the hole was just above a large, empty bucket. Then Remember brought pails of water and, standing on a stool, poured the water into the barrel until it began to drip down through the ashes and the straw into the bucket below. It looked rather dirty as it filtered down into the bucket but Remember took good care not to touch it with her fingers for she knew that it had turned into lye. Late in the afternoon, Remember took out a hen's egg and dropped it into the bucket to see what would happen.

"It floats!" she said. "Now I am sure that I made the lye right and I can attend to the grease tomorrow."

Remember had to start a huge fire the next day. Then she got out the great black soap kettle, filled it with the lye, and hung it over the fire. Into this, she put many scraps of meat fat and waste grease that her mother had been saving for just such a soap-making emergency as this. It bubbled and boiled, and Remember carefully skimmed from the top all the bones and skin and pieces of candle wicking that rose, as the lye absorbed the grease. She cooked it into a thick, ropy mixture that looked very much like molasses candy as it boiled. After a while, Remember knew that it was done. She lifted the kettle off the fire and poured the thick, brown jelly, which was now good soft soap, into big earthenware crocks to cool.

"I made the soap quite as well as my mother could," Remember said to herself with much satisfaction as she put the crocks, all save one, in the cellar. This one she kept for use in the kitchen.

"There's not another thing that I can think of to do," Remember said now. She looked out of the window at the bleak, bare fields beyond which the November sun was just preparing to set in a flame-colored ball.

"Here it is the afternoon before Thanksgiving Day, and Mother and Father are not home yet—and we haven't anything in the house for a Thanksgiving dinner!" She looked toward the woods now. What was that?

The speck of color that she could see in the narrow footpath between the trees suddenly came nearer, growing larger and brighter all the time. Remember could distinguish the gaudy blanket, bright moccasins, and feather headdress of an Indian. Stalking across the field, he was fast approaching their little log house, which he could easily see from the woods and which seemed to offer him an easy goal.

Remember covered her face with her hands, trying in her terror to think of what she should do.

The bolt on the kitchen door was but a flimsy protection at best. Remember knew that the Indian would be able to wrench it off with one tug of his brawny arm. She knew, too, that it had been the custom of the Indians who were encamped not far off to take the children of the colonists and hold them for a high ransom.

"The white man takes our lands; we take the papoose of the white man," they had threatened, and they were indeed cruel to the children whom they held, especially if their parents took a long time supplying the necessary ransom. Still, it had been so long now since an Indian had been seen in their little settlement that Remember's mother had felt safe in leaving her.

Remember looked for a place to hide. There was none. The cellar would be the first place, she knew, where the Indian would look for her. The tall clock was too small a space into which to squeeze her fat little body; and there was no use hiding under the bed for she would be dragged out at once. Remember turned, now hearing a footstep. The Indian—big, brown, and frowning—had crossed the threshold and stood in the center of the room. His blanket trailed the floor; over his shoulder was slung a pair of wild turkeys he had killed.

Remember trembled, but she faced him bravely.

"How!" she said, reaching out a kind little hand to him. The Indian shook his head, and did not offer to shake hands with the little girl. Instead, he pointed to the door, motioning to her that she was to follow him.

Remember's mind worked quickly. She knew that Indians were fond of trinkets and could sometimes be turned away from their cruel designs with very small gifts. She ran to her mother's work basket and offered him in succession a pair of scissors, a case of shiny needles, a scarlet pincushion, and a silver thimble. Each, in turn, the Indian refused, shaking his head and still indicating by his gestures that Remember was to follow him.

Now he grasped the little girl's hand and tried to pull her. There was no use resisting. But just as they reached the door, the Indian caught sight of the crock of soft soap—dark, sticky, and strangely fascinating to him. He stuck one long brown finger in it and started to put it in his mouth, but Remember reached up and pulled his hand away. She shook her head and made a wry face to show him that it was not good to eat.

"How?" he questioned, pointing to the soap.

Remember pulled from his grasp. Pouring a dipper full of water in a basin, she took a handful of the soap and showed the Indian how she could wash her hands. As he watched, first in wonder, and then in pleasure, a smile crept into his face. He smiled and looked at his own hands. They were stained with earth and sadly in need of washing. Remember refilled the basin with

water; and the Indian, helping himself to a huge handful of soap, washed his hands solemnly as though it were a kind of ceremony.

As Remember watched him, her heart beat fast indeed. "As soon as he finishes he will take me away," she thought.

Slowly the Indian dried his hands on the towel she gave him. Then he picked up the crock of soft soap. He set it on his shoulder. Pointing to the pair of turkeys that he had laid on the table to show that he was giving them to Remember in exchange for the soap, he strode out of the door and was soon lost to sight in the wood's path.

Remember dropped down in a chair and could scarcely believe she was really safe. A quick clatter of hoofs roused her. She darted to the door.

"Father, Mother!" she cried.

Yes, it was really her parents. Her father was riding on his horse with her mother in the saddle behind.

"Just in time for Thanksgiving!" they cried as they jumped down and hugged Remember.

"And I'm here, too, and we have a pair of turkeys for dinner," Remember said, half smiles and half tears, as she told them her strange adventure.

Comprehension Questions

1. Why did Remember's mother need to leave her home for several days?

2. What household cleaner did Remember make while her parents were gone?

3. What gift did the Indian take from Remember?

4. Why did Indians sometimes take children away from their parents during the colonial times?

5. Copy the little hymn that Remember sang to herself in the story.

Chapter 4

The Iron Stove

"Did you see him today?" asked a little girl in gray, all excited, as she opened the door to admit her brother.

The boy, shaking with the cold—for it was winter and his jacket was none too thick—set down his basket on the rough wood table and leaned over the tiny fire that burned on the hearth. His eyes shone, though, as he turned to answer his sister.

"Yes, Beth, I saw him down at the wharf and he gave me this." As he spoke, William drew from underneath his coat, where he had tucked it to surprise Beth, a crude little broom made of rushes bound together with narrow strips of willow.

"What is it?" Beth took the broom in her hands and held it up to the light, looking at it curiously. She made a quaint picture in the shifting light of the fire, a little Quaker girl of old Philadelphia, her yellow curls tucked inside a close-fitting gray cap, and her straight gray frock reaching almost to the heels of her heavy shoes.

"It is something new for cleaning," William explained. He took the broom and began sweeping up the ashes on the hearth, as Beth watched him curiously. "Mr. Franklin brought a whole bunch of them down to the wharf to show to people, and he gave me one."

"How did he make it?" Beth asked curiously.

"It took him a whole year, for it had to grow first," William explained. "He saw some brush baskets last year that the sea captains had brought fruit in, lying soaking wet on the wharf. They had sprouted and sent out shoots, so what did Mr. Franklin do but plant the shoots in his garden. They grew and this year he had a fine crop of 'broom corn,' as he called it. He dried it, and bound it into these long-handled brooms."

The children's mother had come in now from the next room and she grasped the hearth broom with eagerness.

"It is just what Philadelphia, the city of cleanliness, needs," she said, as she went to work brushing the corners of the window sills and the mantle piece. "If we were to take more thought of our houses and less of these street brawls regarding who is for and who is against the king, it would be better."

"That is what Mr. Franklin does," William said. "Do you remember how the streets were full of quarreling folk last summer, and a hard thunderstorm came up that everyone thought was sent directly from the skies as a punishment for our wickedness? The women and children were crying, and the men praying when Mr. Franklin came in their midst. I can see him now, look-

ing like a prophet with his long hair flowing over his shoulders and his long cloak streaming out behind him. As the skies flashed with lightning and the thunder crashed, he told them not to be afraid. He said that he would give them lightning rods to put on their houses that would keep them from burning down."

"Yes," their mother said. "He helps us all very much. Mr. Franklin is truly our good neighbor in Philadelphia."

As her mother finished speaking, Beth emptied the basket that William had brought in. There was not a great deal in it—a little flour, some tea, a very tiny package of sugar, and some potatoes. She arranged them on the shelves in the kitchen, shivering a little as she moved around the cold room.

Philadelphia was a new city, and these settlers from across the sea had brought little with them to make their lives cheerful. Outside, huge piles of snow drifted in the narrow streets and were banked on the low stone doorsteps of the small red brick houses. A chilly wind blew up from the wharfs and beat against the bent bodies of the Quakers as they wrapped their long cloaks closely around them.

It was almost as cold in the Arnolds' house as it was outside. The children's father had not been able to stand the hardships of the new country, and there were only Beth, William, and their mother left to face this winter. Mrs. Arnold did fine sewing, and William ran errands for the sailors and merchantmen down at the wharfs, having his basket filled with food in return for his work. It was a hard winter for them, though; no one could deny that.

Mrs. Arnold pulled her chair up to the fireplace now and opened her bag of sewing. Beth leaned over her shoulder as she watched her mother's thin white fingers try to fly in and out of the white cloth.

"Your fingers are stiff with the cold," Beth exclaimed as she blew the coals with the bellows and then rubbed her mother's hands.

"Not very," she tried to smile.

"Yes, very," William said as he swung his arms and blew on his fingertips. "We're all cold. It would be easier to work if we could only keep warm."

Just then they heard a knock at the brass knocker of their door. Beth ran to open it, and both children shouted with delight as a strange, slightly stooping figure entered. His long white hair made him look like some old patriarch. His forehead was high, and his eyes deep set in his long, thin face. His long cloak enfolded him like a mantle. He reached out his toil-hardened hands to greet the family.

"Mr. Franklin!" their mother exclaimed. "We are most glad to see you. You are our very welcome guest always, but it is poor hospitality we are able to offer you. Our fire is very small and the house cold."

"A small fire is better than none," their guest said, "and the welcome in the Arnolds' house is always so warm that it makes a fire unnecessary. Still," he looked at the children's blue lips and pinched cheeks, "I wish that your hearth were wider."

He walked to the fireplace, feeling the bricks and measuring with his eye the breadth and depth of the opening in the chimney. He seemed lost in thought for a moment, and then his face suddenly shone with a smile—a smile like the one it had worn when he had

seen the first green shoots of the broom corn pushing their way up through the ground of his garden.

"What is it, Mr. Franklin?" Beth asked. "What do you see up in our chimney?"

"A surprise," the good neighbor of Philadelphia replied. "If I make no mistake in my plans, you will see that surprise soon. In the meantime, be of good cheer."

He was gone as quickly as he had come, but he had left a glow of cheerfulness and love behind him. All Philadelphia was warmed in this way by Benjamin Franklin. Whenever he crossed a threshold, he brought the spirit of comfort and helpfulness to the house.

"What do you suppose he meant?" Beth asked, as the door closed behind the quaint figure of the man.

"I wonder," William said. Then he took out his speller and copy book, and the words of their visitor were soon forgotten.

But all Philadelphia soon began to wonder at the doings at the big white house where Benjamin Franklin lived. The neighbors were used to hearing busy sounds of hammering and tinkering coming from the back, where Mr. Franklin had built himself a workshop. Recently, however, he had sent away for a small forge;

and now its flying sparks could be seen, and the sound of its bellows heard in the stillness of the long, cold winter nights. Great slabs of iron were unloaded for him at the wharf, and for days no one saw him. He was shut up in his workshop. From morning until night, passers-by heard ringing blows on iron coming from the workshop, as though it were the shop of some country blacksmith.

"Benjamin Franklin wastes his time," said some of the Philadelphians. "He should be in the town hall, helping us to settle some of our land disputes."

But others spoke more kindly of the man of helpful hands.

"Mr. Franklin is making Philadelphia truly a City of Friends by being the best friend of us all," they said.

None could explain Benjamin Franklin's present occupation, though.

In the middle of the winter, Beth and William and their mother went to a friend's house to stay for a week. Mrs. Arnold was not well, and their own house was very cold. The week for which they were invited lengthened into two, then three.

"We must go home," Mrs. Arnold said at last. "Mr. Franklin said that he would stop this afternoon and help William carry the carpet bag. It is time that we began our work again."

As they took their homeward way through the snow, they noticed, again, the happy smile on Mr. Franklin's kind face. He held the handle of the bag with one hand

and Beth's chilly little fingers with the other. He was the spryest of them all as they hurried on. They understood why, as they opened the door of their home.

They started at first, wondering if by any chance they had come to the wrong house. No, there were the familiar things just as they had left them: the row of shining copper pans on the wall, the polished candlesticks on the mantel piece, the warming pan in the corner, and the braided rag rugs on the floor. But the house was as warm as summer. They had never felt such comforting heat in the wintertime before. The fireplace that had been all too tiny was gone. In its place, against the chimney, was a crude iron stove, partly like a fireplace in shape, but with a top and sides that held and spread the heat of the glowing fire inside until the whole room glowed with it.

"That is my surprise," Mr. Franklin explained, rubbing his hands with pleasure as he saw the wonder and delight in the faces of the others, "an iron angel to drive out the cold and frighten away the frost. You can cook on it, or hang the kettle over the coals. It will keep the coals alive all night and not eat up as much fuel as your drafty fireplace did. This is my winter gift to you, my dear friends."

"Oh, how wonderful! How can we thank you for it? We, who were so poor, are the richest family in Philadelphia now. How I shall be able to work!" the children's mother said.

Beth and William extended their hands to catch the friendly warmth of the fire in this, the first stove, in the

City of Friends. It warmed them through and through. Then William examined its rough mechanism so that he would be able to tend it; and Beth bustled about the room, filling the shining brass teakettle and putting a spoonful of tea in the pot to draw a cup for their mother and Mr. Franklin. At last she turned to him, her blue eyes looking deep in his.

"You are so good to us," Beth said. "Why did you work so hard to invent and make this iron stove for us?"

The kindest friend that old Philadelphia ever had stopped a second to think. He never knew the reason for his good deeds. They were as natural as the flowering of the broom corn in his garden. At last he spoke:

"Because of your warm hearts, my friends," he said. "Not that they needed any more heat, but that you may see their glow reflected in the fires you kindle in my stove."

And so may we feel the kindly warmth of Benjamin Franklin's heart in our stoves, which are so much better, but all modeled after the one he made for his neighbors in the Quaker city of long ago.

Chapter 5

The Deacon's Grasshopper

On their way to and from school, the boys and girls of old Boston cast curious glances toward the shop of Deacon Shane Drowne.

It was over two hundred years ago, and they were Colonial children. The boys wore short coats and long trousers, and the little girls long, plain skirts almost touching the tops of their shoes. When it rained, as it often did during the long chilly days of late winter, they wrapped themselves in heavy capes and "ran between the drops," for they had no umbrellas.

But rain or no rain, Samuel, Abigail, and the others could not pass the deacon's tiny window. Through it, they knew they might have a peep at his strange craft. Even the sound of his hammer thrilled them.

He was a coppersmith of old Boston, and his one room shop was down near the wharfs where British ships lay at anchor and the fishermen worked all day. On Sundays, Deacon Drowne went to the white

45

meeting-house on the Common and passed the contribution basket, and he rapped the head of any child who went to sleep during the sermon.

When Monday came, though, the deacon was a very different person. He put on a little round cap and a short leather apron. He perched himself upon a stool beside his work bench and chuckled like a schoolboy as he looked at his sheets of copper and brass, his scissors, dies, and the many hammers—large and small— which he used for shaping metals.

The trade of a coppersmith was not one to interest children greatly in those days. The deacon had to patch some housewife's preserving kettle or make copper toes for the shoes of a little Colonial lad who had worn out the leather too soon to suit his father's sense of economy. Sometimes he had a clock to mend or a teakettle that needed a new handle.

None of these tasks were unusual enough to attract the boys and girls of Boston. They were familiar with teakettles, having to fill them so often, and copper toes on their shoes. It was something quite different that drew them to the window and door of the coppersmith.

"What do you suppose Deacon Drowne will have hidden under his work bench today?" Samuel would ask.

"Oh, I do not know. I am curious to see. Is he not a person of great skill and many surprises?" Abigail would reply.

It was quite true. The old coppersmith saw possibilities in his craft that would have amazed his patrons who thought that the deacon's mind was spent all day long on patches and wires. When his day's work was over, the old coppersmith closed his shutter and lighted a candle. He lighted, too, a small stove in which he could heat his metals and weld them into strange and curious shapes. It seemed to him that the sheets of copper and brass in which he worked were too beautiful for the commonplace uses to which he had to put them.

His mind went back to the days of his boyhood in England when he lived on a farm near the sea and could watch the ships beyond the fields—where the sea lay, blue and clear. As these thoughts came to

him, he welded his metals to make the figures that his memory painted for him. No wonder the children were excited at what the coppersmith would show them that he had made overnight!

He would beckon to them to cross his threshold. Then, with his eyes twinkling like stars through his spectacles, he would hold up in triumph something that he had made. Once it was a little brass rooster, shining and beautiful from his comb to the last tail feather. Once the deacon showed the children a curious little admiral made of copper and holding a telescope as he looked far off at an imaginary sea. Then, to please them, he made a small Indian of copper; the figure was complete even to the feathers in his headdress.

How the children did laugh, though, when Deacon Drowne showed them a copper grasshopper that he had welded! It was so much larger than a real grasshopper that it looked like some strange dragon. It almost filled the tiny shop, its long slender legs stretching in every direction.

"Why did you make it?" the children asked.

The old coppersmith chuckled as he proudly replied, "To show what can be done with my shining metal. It took skill to bend those legs and make the veins in a grasshopper's wings."

"What will you do with it, Deacon Drowne?" asked the children.

The old man shook his head. "Maybe it has no use," he said, looking sadly at the copper grasshopper sprawled out before him.

That was what the sober people of Boston thought, too, all except Mr. Peter Faneuil.

No one could quite understand Mr. Peter Faneuil. He had inherited quite a fortune, but he lived in a simple way and was fonder of children and the sea than of wearing fine broadcloth and having a coach. He joined the children one day, when they went to Deacon Drowne's shop, and saw the grasshopper. They had thought that Mr. Peter Faneuil would laugh at it. He did not even smile. He looked at the shining copper wings and the delicate workmanship of the slim legs. Then he grasped the coppersmith's toil-hardened hand.

"It is a wonderful piece of work," he said. "It should be placed where everyone in Boston could see it."

The deacon smiled with happiness as Mr. Faneuil and the children left him. He touched the grasshopper's perfectly shaped head.

"How could that be?" he said wonderingly.

❖ ❖ ❖

The years went on, and at last no one heard Deacon Drowne's hammering, for he was too old to work any longer at his trade. The children grew up, and Samuel graduated from Harvard College. He was called Samuel Adams now and was quite an influential young man in Boston. He was one of those called to attend a meeting in Boston at which an important decision was to be made.

Should, or should not, Boston accept a gift that Mr. Peter Faneuil wished to make the city from his boundless wealth? He wished to build a public hall in Boston. But this was the unusual part of his wish: the hall was to have a market on the ground floor where the housewives of Boston might come to buy the fruits, tea, and cloth that the merchant ships brought to the city. On the top of the hall there was to be a high tower, and on top of the tower a weathervane that the sailors could see at quite a distance from shore.

"Where shall we transact our important business in this hall?" the meeting members asked Mr. Peter Faneuil.

"In a room over the market," was his quick reply.

Then they argued the question and wrangled about it. A market in a public building did not seem fitting to them, even though there was no public market in Boston at that time. Neither did a weathervane on top of the tower seem suitable. Some were for it, but more were against it. It did not matter that the hall was to be a freewill gift to Boston. They wished no new ideas to break in upon the old ones that belonged to England and the king.

Samuel Adams and his friends were opposed to the idea, but suddenly Mr. Peter Faneuil sent a message to Samuel that made him smile and change his mind. The meeting closed, and the day was carried for Mr. Peter Faneuil. He was to build his hall just as he wished and give it to Boston.

Everyone watched the hall being built with great excitement. It looks like a low, humble enough building now, but it seemed quite large in old Boston. The people who had been opposed to it grew to like it when they realized how much they had needed a market. The magistrates and other officers of the town found that they could hold their meetings quite as well over the market as downstairs. They could come down and help their good wives carry home the day's dinner when they had finished with more weighty matters.

Everyone liked the weathervane. It could be seen for a long distance on land or sea, and its arrow never failed

to fly north, south, east, or west. At first, all Boston was puzzled by the figure on the top of the weathervane. It was different from any that they had ever seen. Persons came from a distance by stagecoach to see it. It shone and glittered in the sunlight.

"Who made it?" the people of Boston asked, and when they found out, the maker was acclaimed as almost a hero.

Patient old Deacon Drowne! He lived long enough to look up through his spectacles and see his great copper grasshopper perched on top of the weathervane of Faneuil Hall.

The grasshopper is there today. It has been on Faneuil Hall since 1742. It saw the Boston Tea Party and heard the shots of the Lexington farmers. It heard the hoof beats of Paul Revere's horse and the splash of the oars of the British troops, rowing into Boston

Harbor. It watched battle and ruin and then saw the coming of peace and plenty again.

Thousands of storms have beaten against its copper wings and legs, but the good workmanship of the old coppersmith has helped the grasshopper to withstand them all. It has been replated and strengthened in places, but the main part of the figure remains just as Deacon Drowne made it—an emblem of the humble, preserved in all its beauty for over two centuries.

Comprehension Questions

1. How did Deacon Shane Drowne make his living?

2. Who bought the copper grasshopper from Deacon Drowne?

3. Did this copper grasshopper ever serve any useful purpose? If so, what purpose did it serve?

4. In what town was Faneuil Hall built?

5. What was Faneuil Hall used for after it was built?

Chapter 6

Patience Arnold's Sampler

"Count your threads, Patience, child. You will do well to pay more attention to your sewing than to looking out the window. It seems that your eyes have been following the garden path quite often the last half-hour, and your work has suffered a great deal.

"Why, when I was a lass in Devon, I had stitched six samplers before I was your age; and one of them had the entire Lord's Prayer upon it embroidered in letters of red so small that your grandma had to wear her glasses in order to spell it out.

"Ah, well, the girls of today are catching the spirit of the times—revolt against the old order and little concern with the new. I must be off, Patience, and cross the orchard to Mistress Edwards's with a bowl of curds. She thinks that they cure her gout. Please attend to your work while I am gone. The sampler is almost finished. I can read the text at the top in spite of its crooked letters, dear child:

'A Soft Answer Turneth Away Wrath.'

"Here are all the letters of the alphabet, too, and now you only need to embroider the name in the correct cross-stitch. Measure your stitches with great care, for you will probably begin it so near the border that you will have little space left for the Arnold name.

"I shall be back by tea time," said Mistress Arnold. Smiling, she stooped to touch with one thin, white hand—stripped of all its jewels—the bowed, brown head of the little girl who sat by the window sewing.

"If you finish the sampler by five o'clock, you may go out in the garden and play. Oh—"

Mistress Arnold turned in the doorway and pulled from her green apron a long iron key.

"I will leave the key to the barn in your charge, Patience, and on no account give it to anyone until I return. Your father tells me that his store of powder and shot is increasing daily, and we are likely to need these soon."

Mistress Arnold sighed as she stepped over the threshold and walked away. Her tall, straight figure in gray clothing glided between the pink clouds that the apple blooms made, and then faded out of sight.

Patience Arnold, a small brown-eyed girl who had seen eight summers in the quaint, white-walled town of Lexington, watched her mother. Then she leaned back in the stiff, wooden chair that was much too high for her, and gave a weary little sigh. It was very dull indeed, to stay in the bare kitchen. All outdoors, the first bees, the robins, and the perfume of the apple trees called her. Oh, if she might only drop her sewing to the floor, and run out to the garden, darting in and out among the trees like a bluebird in her straight frock of indigo-dyed homespun. If she might only sing in her sweet, clear voice, above the hum of bees and birds, the songs that her mother knew—the songs of merry old England, where everyone was happy and everything was delightful!

But, no, she must not go. There was the square of rough cloth in her hand, the sticky needle, and the thread that would knot despite Patience's care. Every little girl in Lexington had finished a sampler, and some of them two, by the time they were nine. She must hurry, for the afternoon was wearing away. Soon the sun would drop behind the orchard, and she had a long name to sew—Patience Arnold.

Patience took up her needle again and began to count the stitches and embroider the letters, P, A, T. There were so many letters, and they marched across the cloth almost as crookedly as the new minutemen whom her father drilled on the village green when it was dusk. No one saw the minutemen march and countermarch, and no one could hear their feet in the soft grass. Patience laughed to herself as she bent over the letters of her work and pictured the new soldiers who were learning to march.

"You are Mistress Anderson's lad who has such long legs and thinks he will be the captain of the militia some day," said Patience as she pointed to the A.

"And you—" She put her needle in the T.

A moment later, however, a long shadow lay across the doorsill. There were other shadows on the grass outside. Where had they come from? Why, the orchard was full of soldiers. One stood, even now, in front of Patience—a most gallant gentleman in scarlet broadcloth and gold lace, holding his cocked hat in his hand and smiling down at the little girl.

"So the bumpkins of this little town of Lexington, too, have taken upon themselves the gentle art of soldiering. It is high time that his Majesty interfered."

The man seemed to speak to himself. Then he bent so low over the little girl in her straight-backed chair that the gilt fringe which dangled from his epaulets brushed Patience's cheek.

"Such a pretty little lass, and so industrious as she sits alone in this great house."

He paused, watching Patience's trembling little white fingers. She was frightened by this soldier of the King of England. Then he continued, "I need shelter for my men."

He pointed to a group of soldiers in red coats who swarmed the dooryard now, laughing, brawling, and trampling on Mistress Arnold's garden of savory herbs.

"The day is warm, and we have had a long march from Boston town. I would like my men to lie and rest a while on the cool hay of your barn, my little lady. We have tried the door, but we find it locked, and the key

is missing from the padlock. Will you give me the key, little maid?"

Patience bent lower over her work as the last words came from the man's lips. Reaching in her homespun pocket for the key which her mother had given her, she clasped it in her hand and held it underneath the sampler as she stitched the letters once more. For a second she did not speak. It seemed as though her throat was burning. Her lips were dry with fear. Then she looked up, smiling a wistful little smile.

"No, kind sir. I cannot give you the key."

"Oh, so the little lady is stubborn," said the soldier.

The man crossed to the door and motioned to the waiting soldiers outside. In a second they obeyed his summons, swarming Mistress Arnold's clean kitchen and covering the spotless floor with the dust of the dirt road.

"Search the house!" commanded their leader. "This little rebel girl is tongue-tied and stubborn. She will neither give up the key, nor tell me where it is. Overturn the chests of drawers; tear up the carpets, break down the doors, spare nothing, I say, but bring me the key to the barn."

No sooner were the words spoken than the work of destruction began. Sounds of doors and hinges wrenched from their places, the tramp of rough boots on the floor above her head, the rattle of chests told the frightened little Patience that the work of searching the house had begun. It seemed to her that the key would burn its way straight through her palm. Her hands trembled, and her eyes filled with tears so that she could scarcely see her needle. But still she stitched, never leaving her chair, nor lifting her white little face.

The soldier who had given the command remained in the kitchen, pacing restlessly up and down, his arms folded, and a frown deepening on his forehead. "P. A. T. I. E. N."–Patience was nearing the edge of the sampler, and it was with difficulty that she stitched because of the key that lay underneath the cloth. The letters were crooked and straggling, and lacking the precision of even those who were untrained minutemen. There was no sound in the room now, except the ticking of a tall clock and the tread of the soldier's feet.

Suddenly, the soldier in command stopped in front of Patience's chair and laid a heavy hand on her little arm. He spoke, and the words were full of anger.

"Enough of this nonsense! Give me the key, I say. I will have it!"

Patience slipped out of her chair and down to the floor, holding her sampler, covering the hidden key, as high as the man's eyes. He loosed his grasp upon her arm, looking at her in wonder. Such a little girl, in her straight blue frock, and not as tall as his own little girl in England. She had the same soft eyes, though, and the same low, sweet voice.

"I would gladly give you what you wish, sir," she began bravely, "but I promised my mother I would deliver the key to no one until she returned. Look!" She held the sampler still higher. "I am stitching my name. Is it not a boring task on such a pretty day?"

"A soft answer turneth away wrath." The man read the text at the top of the sampler. Then he looked out of the window and stared at the apple trees outside.

"It is truly neatly stitched, little girl," he said. "My own daughter Elizabeth is also making her sampler, and wetting it with tears until I return to her, overseas."

He gave a quick command to his men, who walked down the stairs, empty-handed, and into the garden. Then he raised his hat in salute and followed them as they marched slowly down the road until Patience could no longer see any soldiers.

"My little girl—my Patience—are you safe?"

It was Mistress Arnold who ran across the orchard and into the kitchen, clasping the trembling little girl in her arms. "We saw the Redcoats from Mistress Edwards's window and knew that they had been here. But you are unharmed—and the guns—the powder?"

"I spoiled my sampler, Mother." Patience gave a sobbing laugh as she held up her work with the crookedly stitched ending and the unfinished name. "It is as you feared. I started my name too near the border and there is no room to finish it." Then she held out the precious piece of iron and said, "But, here is the key."

63

Chapter 7

The Star Lady

The following letter is from Tabitha Wells, age ten, who lived in Philadelphia, in the year 1776, to her cousin John Bradford in Boston.

My Dear John:

It does seem more than a month ago that I said good-bye to you, and you took your long journey home again. Your visit was a bright spot in these troubled times. Do you remember the pair of robins that we watched building their nest in Grandmother's old apple tree? They have raised their brood of young ones now, and the little birds have flown away. The old birds still live in the apple tree, though; and, each day at sunrise and sunset, they sing as if all the world were joyful instead of fallen into this sad Revolution. And the early apples are as red as the coat of a British soldier and are dropping all over the grass of the garden.

Grandmother gave me a pewter canister that used to hold tea—she knew it would be a long time before we have any more tea to put in it. I have filled it full of

apples, one layer of fruit and then one of leaves to keep them from bruising. It is as sweet smelling as our garden, John, where you played with me so many happy days this spring. It is for you; the apples shall go to you by the next mail package.

I hope you can forgive me for writing to you about such everyday matters as robins and apples, wasting paper which is rising in price, and using up one of my grandfather's best quill pens and his ink bowl. I had other things in mind to tell you, John, when I started this letter—things of far greater importance.

Strange things have happened to your cousin Tabitha Wells in Philadelphia since she said good-bye to you, John. I feel as though I, a little girl of only ten summers and not as learned as I should be, should take part in these great and stirring times in the Colonies.

And now, my dear John, I will tell you about what has been happening to me.

I think that we played so much at home when you visited me, John, that I had no time to take you to the little upholstery shop on Arch Street, near Grandmother's house, which is my special delight.

It is run by Mistress Betsy Ross, who is not much more than a grown-up girl. They say she is just past twenty years in age, and she has a great pleasure in letting me visit and watch her at work. Her husband was a brave young patriot in our American Colonies who was killed a short time ago. Mistress Betsy Ross always helped him in his shop; now that he is dead, she must carry on the work of the shop herself. Thankfully, Mistress Ross is very talented with a needle and thread.

When I have finished wiping the silverware after lunch, I ask Grandmother if I can go down for the rest of the afternoon to the shop of Mistress Betsy. I think that we are both lonely; I, the only child in my house because my father left me when he joined the army; and she a slim, sweet lady, all alone in her shop.

Such pretty materials she has, John! If you were a girl, your eyes would stick out with envy, and your fingers ache for scissors and needle. She gave me a piece of yellow satin brocade, picked out with a pattern of butterflies. I made a court dress with it for my wooden doll—although Grandmother says such finery is not for a doll even in these days.

But here I am letting my pen go wandering again, John. It is not about my doll that I am minded to write you, but of the important thing that happened in the shop of Mistress Betsy Ross this summertime. I was there, John. I saw it with my own eyes.

Mistress Betsy was fitting new covers to Grandmother's best fiddle-backed chairs, and I had come down to her shop to see if they were done. It happened that they were, but I decided to stay for a while for Mistress Betsy was busy doing a special project. She was stitching a flag.

You know of course that each of our American Colonies has its own flag, each of a different design, although they all favor the same colors—red, white, and blue. Such days as these, when troops are marching to war, there is need of many flags, and so Mistress Betsy is as busy stitching them as she is in making her furniture covers. So quick and talented she is, John.

I wish you could see how neatly she sews together the colors, and stitches on the designs. No scrap of cloth is wasted, and each flag that Mistress Betsy makes is always perfect in shape and pattern. I think that the mailman had just brought Mistress Betsy some bundles of fresh stuff for her flag making, red and blue, and she was looking it over as she spoke to me:

"Tabitha, child," Mistress Betsy said to me, "it would save me much time and work if I had one pattern for a flag. It tries my patience to have to remember thirteen different flag patterns."

"I think so, too." The voice of a man surprised us, and we looked up to see a very grand gentleman standing in the door of the shop and looking at us. "I heard your speech just now, Mistress Ross," he said, "and it is even upon such an errand that I come to you. The Continental Congress is of a mind to adopt one flag that will be the flag of freedom and the emblem of the brave; one banner for the Colonies. The fame of your fine needlework has come to our ears, Mistress Ross, and we are here to talk with you about this matter."

The gentleman, very fine indeed in his blue broadcloth and gold lace, stepped into the little shop now, and behind him were other gentlemen in the uniform of the Colonies.

I confess, John, that I was a bit awed, and I hid myself behind the door, where I could hear but not be seen. You see, I was in my linsey-woolsey frock, not dressed for company. Mistress Betsy wore her long working apron over her blue cotton dress, but she curtsied with great ease.

"You honor me, Mr. Washington," Mistress Betsy said. "I have been looking forward to putting my needle into just one flag, and one only. What might be your wishes and that of the Congress in the pattern of this flag?"

So this was the great Mr. Washington! My heart went pit-a-pat, John, as loudly it seemed to me as sounded the ticking of a clock. I tried to remain quiet as I listened to Mr. Washington's every word.

"We have not made any fixed design for an American flag, Mistress Ross," Mr. Washington said. "We feel that all the thirteen colonies should, in some way, be included in it; and I have a great desire that there should be stars."

He took a pen from Mistress Betsy's desk and began making drawings on a piece of paper. Mistress Betsy looked over his shoulder and watched his long fingers, trying to see what manner of a flag he was designing.

"See, Mistress Ross," Mr. Washington said, "I would like stars like this." He held up his drawing.

Mistress Betsy took the drawing and looked at it, turning it first one way, and then the other. I came out from behind the door and looked, too, for I was of a curious mind about this new flag. Oh, John, if you could have seen the strange, crooked star that Mr. Washington had drawn! He is a great soldier and statesman, without doubt, but he is not an artist. I saw Mistress Betsy's eyes twinkle, but she was quite sober and respectful when she spoke.

"You have your eyes on your men, Mr. Washington, during your night marches, not on the stars. Your star is drawn with six points, and it should have only five points. May I be so bold as to show you how to make a five-pointed star?"

Then Mistress Betsy picked up a scrap of white cloth, folded it neatly into five parts, made one snip with her scissors and opened it. There was a perfect star with five points!

Mr. Washington took it, and as he looked at it his stern face changed, and he smiled. Then he bowed as he turned to go.

"Well done, Mistress Ross," he said. "I have the idea of an American flag in my mind, but you have it in your fingers. Put your wits to the task of designing a flag to submit to the Congress, and I hope that the Colonies will see fit to adopt it. Good afternoon, Mistress of Flags!" and Mr. Washington and his gentlemen had gone.

Oh, John, how excited we were then! Mistress Betsy took my hands in hers and she danced like a girl with me about the shop. Then she sat down in her big wooden rocking chair and took me in her lap. She put her arms around me and pulled my head close to hers. I thought she was going to cry as she spoke:

"Tabitha Wells," she said. "The chance has come for me to do something for my country. My husband died for the Colonies, but I, who must live, may perhaps make the flag that will wave in remembrance of him and of all the other patriots!"

And I, knowing how she felt, could only hug her, not speaking because of a large lump in my throat.

But we soon realized that it was not a time for tears, but for work. Mistress Betsy jumped up and thrust her hands deep into her colored stuffs.

"Only three colors for the flag of our country, Tabitha," she said. "Red for the blood of her patriots, blue for her truth, and white for her purity. But now, for the design?" She laid the pieces of cloth together and tried them this way and that.

Oh, how we puzzled our minds, John, over that flag—or Mistress Betsy did, while I looked on and clapped my hands in pride for her. I forgot the time. It grew late, and Grandfather had to come for me; but I went again the next day to Mistress Betsy's shop to watch her plan the pattern of the first American flag.

You see, my dear John, it was no easy task. Mr. Washington had said that he was of a mind to have the thirteen Colonies represented in it. Mistress Betsy, herself, was always of a mind to make her needlework good to look at because of its simplicity. So she cut, stitched, ripped, and then stitched again. It was weary work and lasted through the burning of many candles, but finally Mistress Betsy finished her flag.

Oh, John, if you could only see it! It is plain, which helps to show its bright colors of red, white, and blue. It has seven long red stripes and six long white stripes, making thirteen in all, for the thirteen Colonies. As I look at the stripes they remind me of the long way our Colonies are taking to their freedom. Then, in one corner of the flag is a large piece of blue cloth, and sewed to it with Mistress Betsy's tiny stitches are thirteen stars. The stars are for our Colonies, too. Like stars, they will shine.

And now comes the amazing part of this letter, which has frustrated you, I fear, with all its messy scratching. Mr. Washington is so pleased with Mistress Betsy's endeavor to carry out his wishes that her flag is to be adopted by the Congress. It will be our American flag forever. I, Tabitha Wells, know the sweet lady who made it. I can scarcely wait for my father to come home to tell him about it. The flag of our Union, John, made here in Philadelphia and in the shop of my Mistress Betsy. I am going to call her my Star Lady from now on.

Your patience has been tried, dear John, I fear, in reading this long letter. I have had trouble with my quill pen, which would not travel over the paper as fast as my thoughts came. I hear that you are having stirring times in Boston, and I pray that you are safe and well. I shall count the days until your next letter comes to me in the mail.

As soon as I can, I will have a small flag made for you in the Star Lady's shop. Maybe I can send it with the same package as the apples. So, you will remember Philadelphia well, John, by the fruit of our garden and by the first American flag.

Your cousin,
Tabitha Wells

Comprehension Questions

1. Who was the "Star Lady"?

2. What happened to Mistress Ross's husband?

3. In what city did Tabitha Wells live?

4. Who asked Mistress Ross to design and make the first United States flag?

5. Why did the first American flag have thirteen stripes and thirteen stars on it?

Chapter 8

The Flag of Their Regiment

Prudence looked up from her sewing. It was a pleasant place to work, in the morning sunshine that trickled through the big white pillars on the front porch and into the window of her house. The wide street was shaded by the leafy branches of the spreading elms, but the houses that lined the streets were strangely empty of life.

This story took place in Philadelphia many years ago, during the time of the American Revolution. Prudence was a quaint, shy, little Colonial girl. In all her eleven years, she had known nothing but the daily routine of the simple home—the scouring of floors, the polishing of copper kettles and mahogany chairs, the making of huge loaves of bread and yellow butter and round cheeses, the bleaching of linen, and the patching together of bright blocks of colored cloth to make log-cabin and morning-star bed quilts.

Sometimes Prudence would attend a quilting bee or donation party at her local minister's house. These activities, with their feasts of rich preserves and pound cake, and the children's table set after the grown-ups had finished, were wonderful parties for Prudence. Usually, though, her days were plain and simple. She helped her mother and studied her lessons from schoolbooks in strange wooden covers, and stitched her sampler when the studying was done.

It was not a cross-stitch sampler, though, that Prudence was working on so busily now. Her needle flew in and out as she stitched with even, small stitches some long straight strips of red calico and white cotton. In her lap lay some star-shaped pieces of plain white cotton cloth. The edges were neatly turned in and ready to sew upon a square of blue cloth that Prudence had just cut.

"Please stop your work! It's too pleasant a day to sew."

Prudence looked up and saw a boy—her neighbor, William Brewster—standing outside the window. The hair of each of these Philadelphia children was cut short and square. They had the same round, rosy faces. Prudence's long-sleeved, full-length dress and William's ruffled shirt were both cut from the same cloth. It was grayish-green cloth from Deacon Wells's store. From beneath William's trousers and Prudence's dress showed the same stout shoes with copper tips on the toes. William reached through the window and pulled at Prudence's sewing.

"Oh, William!" Prudence gasped. "Be careful; you'll soil the white cotton cloth. What happened to your hands? I never saw them so stained before in all my life." William stepped back from the window and held up his two dirty brown hands in the sunlight, laughing merrily.

"You are right, Prudence," he said. "My hands need a dose of my mother's good soft soap, but"—the boy's voice dropped to a whisper—"all this morning I have been busy digging holes in the orchard."

"Why?" Prudence's blue eyes were wide with wonder. William stepped closer now and looked all about him to see that no one was listening. Then he whispered in Prudence's ear.

"For burying the silver," he explained. "We packed it all in a strong box—my grandmother's teaspoons, the silver cake basket with the design of strawberries around the edge, and the sugar tongs. We buried them all, oh, very deeply."

"Was it necessary, William?" Prudence's eyes were frightened as she spoke. "I know that my mother, before she had to rest in her bed with a broken ankle, planned to hide our silver in the dry well that is in our yard. Are—are the Redcoats coming through Philadelphia soon?"

"They do say that they are coming. I am very fearful," William answered. Then, as Prudence's pink cheeks grew a little pale at the thought, the boy pointed to her sewing. "What are you stitching, Prudence? Surely you are not going to dress yourself in these gaudy colors during these hard times?"

Prudence laughed, shaking out the strips of scarlet and white that filled her lap. "No, William. Dark colors and plain coats must be worn by us children of the war. I am making a flag. Our great, beautiful stars and stripes of the Colonies went to our regiment with father and your brother John. But I went down to the flag shop of Mrs. Betsy Ross not long ago, and I stood awhile on the threshold, watching how she and her maids cut and sewed their red, white, and blue cloth together. I said to myself, 'Why not make your own flag, Prudence Williams? You have ten fingers and a sewing bag up in the attic.' And here it is, all done except for sewing on the little white stars."

"Oh, Prudence!" William's eyes shone. "It is wonderful! How did you ever measure and sew it so well? I

always did say that you are the most clever girl with your needle of any in town."

"It is carefully made," Prudence assented, "but that is because I thought of my regiment with every stitch. And I wished that I might march in the regiment beside my father, waving my flag, and shouting for the independence of our dear Colonies with every step. Oh, it is hard, William, to be a child during the Revolutionary War, with nothing to do but sit at home."

"That it is," William said, "but now let's go in the house and reach into your cookie jar, Prudence. Maybe your cook has filled it with her good caraway muffins." The two little neighbors disappeared into the kitchen.

◈　　◈　　◈

In the days that followed, Prudence completely forgot that the British soldiers were coming to Philadelphia. Rumors came of how the Redcoats had marched through the nearby towns and countryside. They had taken items from the homesteads, stolen the supplies that had been left for the women and children, and plundered the treasure of silver that belonged to the Colonists. News of this reached the ears of those who remained behind—alone, in Philadelphia.

Prudence paid little heed to the rumors, however. Her mother was better, but she was still an invalid and confined to her room. There was only one maid servant to do work in the large house, and Prudence found herself a real little housekeeper with her hands very busy. All day long she tripped up and down the wide oak staircase with instructions from her dear mother to the maid in the kitchen, and then Prudence helped to carry them out.

She had finished the flag and put it away in a drawer. "It's hardly safe to fly a flag from your front porch,

Prudence," sensible William had warned. So Prudence opened the drawer only when she had a little spare time. Then she would kneel down on the rag carpet in front of the drawer and hold the beloved Stars and Stripes tenderly in her arms. "I love every star, and every color," she would say to herself. "Oh, may God win the battle for us and help to give me back my father, and William his brother John!"

One morning, when Prudence set the tray with her mother's breakfast, she prepared it with unusual care. Upon the sun-bleached linen cloth stood the thin china dishes, white with a pattern of grapes in purple and green. The silver spoons and forks were arranged neatly. Prudence's mother, sitting in a big arm chair by the window, where the sweet odors of the garden roses were blown up to her, looked lovingly at her small daughter.

"You are a good little housewife, my dear," she said. "I don't know what I would have done without you. Father will find his little girl almost a little woman when he returns." She paused a moment, lifting one of the silver spoons to break the end of her eggshell. "If he ever does return," she sighed. "Oh, I should have hidden the silver weeks ago." The sound of a muffled drum struck her ear. She looked at Prudence in terror. "Pull the curtains closed, child, and lock all the doors. The Redcoats are coming."

Like a line of fire taking its winding way in and out between the houses, the regiment of British soldiers streamed through the streets of Philadelphia. Here, it stopped as an officer and his men stripped the fruit from some peaceful orchard or garden. There, at an officer's order, a group of soldiers entered a house, and returned with bits of old family treasure that war gave them the chance to steal.

Prudence's heart beat fast, but she tried to be brave. She ran from room to room, stowing away the silver candlesticks and tableware, closing blinds, and locking doors. The old maid servant, her apron held over her head, had fled to the cellar in fear. Her mother, bravely directing Prudence, was still unable to leave her room.

Suddenly, the front door burst open and in came William. "I couldn't bear to leave you alone, Prudence," he said. "See, I brought my father's old drum, thinking we could make a little noise on it and scare the Redcoats."

Prudence studied the brave face of her little neighbor. "You've given me an idea, William," she exclaimed. She ran over to the chest of drawers, opened one drawer, and pulled out the little homemade flag. "We'll both scare the Redcoats," she said. "We won't fasten the doors, for it wouldn't be of any use. The soldiers could very easily break the bolts, and I can't find any safe place to hide the silver. Come. We'll go right out on the porch and meet the whole British army if it comes!" She clutched William's hand, and tugged him toward the door.

"Do we dare?" William's round, merry face was very sober.

"Of course we dare. Come on. You drum and I'll wave the Stars and Stripes," Prudence said.

The Williams' white house, set a little back from the street in the midst of sweet old flower beds, looked like a prize to the ruthless Redcoats. It was well-known in Philadelphia at that time that Prudence's father had used much of his wealth to further the cause of the Colonies. This made the invading enemy hate him. It was a common rumor, too, that although the Williams' chests of gold were greatly depleted, there was still much treasure of silver left in the home. News of it passed from mouth to mouth among the soldiers.

"There's the house. Left flank, wheel, Halt!" shouted the British general in command. He turned in at the Williams' gate and strode up the path. At the steps he looked up and stopped. "Gad!" he said, "The children of these stubborn Colonists would defy us, too." But a smile took away the stern lines from his mouth.

On the top step of the porch stood Prudence and William, two brave little Colonists. William was beating a loud rap tap, on the cracked head of an old drum. Prudence, her arm held high above her head, waved the little homemade flag that showed the glorious stars and stripes of their regiment. "You mustn't come a step farther, sir!" she commanded.

"No indeed!" echoed William. "We won't let you come in."

"So you're holding the fort, are you?" the general asked.

"We have to, sir," Prudence explained. "My father is with the army of the Colonies and my mother is ill. This is my neighbor, William Brewster. He came over to help me guard the house." Then she turned pleading eyes toward the great man as she held out her flag. "It looks to me as though there are more or less a thousand Redcoats out on the road, sir. There are only two of us. Please, sir, for the sake of our flag, march on!"

Was it dust or the mist of tears that made the British general wipe his eyes? He reached out one ungloved hand and grasped Prudence's little one.

"Give my sympathy to your mother, my child," he said kindly, "and tell her that I hope she will soon be better. Little soldiers, remember that never before have I surrendered, but now I do, in the name of the king. March on!" he ordered his men. Looking back, he saw Prudence and William standing in the gate waving good-bye to him until the trees and the distance shut them from his view.

Chapter 9

The Boy Who Had Never Seen an Indian

"I saw Painted Feathers this morning," the boy said as he threw himself down on the rude log bench in front of the fire and stretched out his hands to feel the blaze. "He seemed angry about something," he went on, "but he and the young braves were glad to see me. They like us, Mother. Painted Feathers remembers how you took care of his little daughter, Laughing Eyes, when she strayed away from the camp up in the Blue Ridge Mountains. He still wears the beads you gave him around his neck. Heap big chief, Painted Feathers, often seems angry but I guess we've made him our friend."

The woman in homespun, who bent over a savory stew brewing in a kettle that hung from the crane, smiled as she looked down at the boy's manly face. He was the counterpart of his father, who had gone hunting over the Blue Ridge, and had never returned—lost in the trackless wilderness of the woods, they feared. He wore the same type of rough suit of tanned skins, hide boots, and fur cap. His eyes were just as deep and fearless as his father's had been. He was his mother's mainstay now in the little cabin, which was set so far from any other habitation in the depth of the wilderness. There were Indians near, but so far they had been friendly to the two settlers.

"I tried to understand what Painted Feathers was angry about," the lad continued.

"What was it, Eli? Nothing that we have done, I trust?" the boy's mother asked, her voice trembling a little as she peered out through the window at the gathering dusk and the gloomy forest that surrounded them.

"Oh, no, Mother," Eli hastened to assure her. "As nearly as I could make out, Painted Feathers and the tribe are afraid of losing their land. They pointed toward the direction of the Shenandoah River, beyond the Blue Ridge, as it flows into the Potomac. They say that the land in that valley is being measured off with strange instruments by white men who are going to bring their own tribes and build their own camps there. You can't blame Painted Feathers, Mother, for his tribe settled here first. I thought, as I came home, what a pity it would be to take the land away from the Indians—such lofty trees, the silver river, and the buds of the wild flowers opening everywhere. I never saw the mountains look so blue as they did in the sunshine this morning, and Painted Feathers has lived here for years and years." Eli's clear, boyish voice was full of sympathy.

"I know, too, how Painted Feathers feels about this valley," Eli's mother said. "He knows every deer track and every spring and partridge call for miles around. But, I think this is all talk about surveyors being near, Son. No one has marked out the lands in all this time, and they would scarcely begin now. How much longer the days are!" she added, turning toward the door to open it and let in the night air. It was early spring and the twilight was long and mellow.

To her surprise, she found a boy standing outside. His hand, which he had raised to knock with, went like a flash to his cap. He pulled it off and stood, bare-headed, as he bowed like a young cavalier and smiled up at her. He was about Eli's age, she thought, between fifteen and sixteen, but a different sort of lad from her sturdy son. His long, pale face had the lines of an aristocrat. Even his slender fingers showed his gentle heritage.

"May I ask shelter of you for the night," he begged courteously. As he spoke, Eli's mother noticed that he carried surveying instruments, and his clothing was weather-stained and worn.

"I have come all the way up the Shenandoah and over the mountains, measuring and marking the land, and making maps of its important features," he said. "I have not slept more than three or four nights in a bed but, after tramping through your wild forests all day, have lain down before a fire on a little straw or bearskin like some beast of the wood. And my cooking has been done on sticks over the same fire with chips of wood for plates." He smiled as he told of the hard-

ships. "I have strayed away from my companions," he said, "and do not know where to spend the night."

Eli, crowding close to his mother in the doorway, had been listening to the tale of the stranger with the greatest interest. He pushed open the door now.

"Come in," he said.

"Yes, you must come in and share our supper, and stop with us in the cabin as long as you like," Eli's mother added. And in a few minutes, the three were gathered around the rough wooden table before the fire, eating bowlfuls of the steaming broth.

"My name is Eli. What is yours?" Eli asked, between mouthfuls.

"George," said the other lad. "I live at Mount Vernon. Our neighbor, Lord Fairfax, has an estate that is so large it extends way over the Blue Ridge Mountains. Ever since I was a little lad, I have ridden and walked with Lord Fairfax; and, when he decided to have his estate surveyed, even as far as this distant boundary, I gladly undertook the work. I like this wild life and the adventure of making new paths in the wilderness."

"Tell me about some of your adventures, George," Eli begged, leaning across the table, his eyes bright with excitement.

"The narrowest escape we had," George replied, "was when we made our straw beds on the ground a few nights ago and were awakened by smelling something scorched. The straw was on fire, and we were almost burned alive."

"Have you seen any Indians?" Eli asked.

"Not an Indian," the young surveyor replied. "Indeed, I wish that I might, for I never have seen an Indian in my life. They were driven out of Virginia long ago, you know, by the Colonists. Once, though," he added, "and not so many days ago, if I remember rightly, we were setting up our stakes around a tract of land near here and we heard a sudden crackling in the bushes. There was a bit of bright color showing among the branches as we looked, like the bright feathers of a chief's head-dress, but it was gone in a moment. It may have been only a scarlet tanager, or a red-headed woodpecker," he said carelessly.

The words had scarcely escaped his lips, though, when a sudden light flashed against the window of the cabin, lighting like day the scene outside. As scarlet and yellow leaves are whirled in a moment by a sudden gust of wind from a forest, so the thirty or more Indians who surrounded the cabin seemed to have flashed out of the woods—as swiftly and as silently. Painted Feathers led them, decked in fresh war paint—as were all the other braves—and a scalp dangled menacingly from his belt to show that he was bent on warfare. With fierce gestures toward the cabin and the three white faces that peered in terror from the window, the Indians made their preparations. One of the younger braves drummed loudly on a deerskin that he had stretched over an iron pot. Another rattled a huge, dried gourd filled with shot and decorated with a horse's tail. The others built a great fire directly in front of the cabin, pulled blazing brands from it, and danced in a circle with wild yells and whoops.

Eli whispered his frightened explanation to the other lad. "It's Painted Feathers and his band of braves, and they're dancing the death dance. When they finish they'll set fire to our cabin, I'm afraid. He used to be our friend, but this morning he seemed in a great rage

about his land and hunting ground being taken away from the tribe by settlers." Eli's voice was trembling as he finished. "It wasn't a wild bird that you heard and saw in the woods when you were surveying, George. It was Painted Feathers watching you, and now he has followed you to our cabin."

The other lad's heart beat with terror, but his voice did not falter as he spoke: "Then I am going out to give myself up to the Indians, Eli. I won't have your life and that of your mother endangered when you have been so kind as to take me, a stranger, into your house and feed and shelter me." He made a quick movement toward the door, but Eli intercepted him.

"Wait, George! It would only satisfy their rage without doing any good. Let me think a moment."

But as the three waited and watched, the cabin lighted by the fire outside, the seconds seemed like hours. The shouting, excited Indians piled more logs upon the fire and fed it with pine knots until the sparks darted in a crimson cloud as high as the tops of the trees. As they danced, they circled nearer and nearer the cabin, their shrieks growing each moment more shrill and menacing. It was time to act if the cabin and its occupants were to be saved. Before either his mother or the boy surveyor could stop him, Eli stepped out in front of the cabin, alone and unprotected. He stood there, one hand extended in welcome to the terrible Indian chief.

The sudden appearance of the boy was a surprise to the Indians. They were silent for a moment, spellbound by the boy's bravery, and interested as well, in something that he drew from his coat and held out in supplication to Painted Feathers. He had grasped the object from its place on the shelf over the fireplace before he left the cabin. It was a tiny moccasin made of the softest of deerskin and embroidered with bright beads. Painted Feathers drew nearer to look, and Eli spoke to him.

"Laughing Eyes left her moccasin in the wigwam of her paleface friends. We kept the moccasin because we love Laughing Eyes. We found her when she strayed away from the tribe and we gave her back to her father, Painted Feathers, the big chief."

As the boy spoke, Painted Feathers nodded his great head slowly, and his cruel face softened a little. Eli was quick to see the advantage that he had gained and he acted upon it.

"A strange paleface has come to the cabin. He measures the land in the valley, but he is the friend of the Indians. He will protect their hunting grounds and keep away strange tribes from the west. Will Painted Feathers say 'How' to the stranger?" Eli asked, his voice trembling because of his bold request.

Painted Feathers held the little moccasin in his hand now, the touch of it warming and softening his stony heart. Then he slowly nodded his head in assent, stalking nearer the cabin door.

"Come, George," cried Eli breathlessly. "Come out and meet your friend, Painted Feathers, the big chief."

In the flaring light of the torches, the great Indian solemnly shook hands with the boy surveyor. Then, as the two boys stood in the doorway, the chief went back to the fire and gave a quick order to the braves. In a second, their fearful death dance was changed to the slow, stately steps of a dance of welcome. At its end, they put out the fire and filed silently back into the forest.

Snuggled under bearskins in front of the warm hearth, the two boys slept but little that night and talked a great deal about their wonderful adventure.

"You needn't be afraid to go in the morning, George," Eli assured the boy surveyor. "Painted Feathers's tribe is the only band of Indians anywhere around here; and, now that he knows you are his friend, he won't harm you."

"I shall never forget you, Eli," said George. "You have taught me how to be brave."

George's companions found him in the morning outside the cabin. With many thanks and assurances of his friendship, the young surveyor left the settlers' cabin and started to finish his work and his trip.

A period of twenty years soon passed. Where the trees had grown, there was a town now, and the cabin itself was replaced by a comfortable frame dwelling. Eli's mother was an old lady and he, a grown man. It was a time of much stress for America, the period of the Revolution.

"Great news, Mother!" Eli exclaimed as he came in one day. "They say that General George Washington has taken Lord Cornwallis and all his army as prisoners. Yorktown has surrendered, and the war is over!"

"General George Washington?" repeated his mother, her mind going back through the years. Then a thought came to her. "Eli," she said, "do you remember the lad surveyor who stayed with us for a night when you were a boy? He told me his full name as he was leaving. I have never thought to tell you his name over the years. George Washington, he said he was."

The man's eyes flashed. "One and the same," he said. "The great general and our guest, George, who had never seen an Indian."

Comprehension Questions

1. What type of work does a surveyor do?

2. Where did George live?

3. Who was Lord Fairfax?

4. How did Eli convince Painted Feathers that he should not burn them to death?

5. Who was Laughing Eyes?

Chapter 10

Richard,
The Youngest Soldier

"Did you hear the news, Richard?" The children on their way to school along the elm-lined street of Hartford caught up with the lad of ten and spoke to him.

"They say that General Burgoyne and all his Redcoats are marching down from Canada and will fight their way to Albany. Our soldiers are dropping out of the ranks from weariness with this long struggle, and General Schuyler is calling for more recruits."

"My father is going to enlist in the Continental Army," said Richard.

"So is my brother," said the other boy.

"And my father, too," said another child.

The lads and lassies in their homespun clothes drew themselves up proudly. They loved this fair, green land of America with its fields of yellow corn and orchards of tasty fruit. They loved its blazing fireplaces, the

games on the Common, and the brave, ragged army of farmer soldiers who were trying to free the Colonies.

"Do you know what General Washington says about us?" Abigail, a quaint little girl in a long dress asked, touching Richard's sleeve. "He says if all the states had done their duty as well as our little State of Connecticut, the war would have been over long ago. But of course that doesn't mean us, Richard," she added. "There's nothing we children can do for the Colonies."

Richard drew himself up proudly. Although he was but ten years old, he could stand straight and hold his head as high as a soldier. He looked down the street toward a big white house with the Stars and Stripes flying from the pole on the green lawn. It was the recruiting station where volunteers were enrolled to march against the Redcoats.

"I should like to help General Washington," he said. "Maybe they would let me enlist."

A shout of laughter went up from the children. "A boy of ten a soldier in the Continental Army!"

"What would you do for your country?" mocked one child.

"All you know, Richard, is how to play tunes on your grandfather's fife," teased another.

The words hurt the little lad and his face flushed. He was about to speak, but the boys and girls scattered, some running ahead swinging their school bags, some stopping to look at the sweets in Mrs. Brewster's bakeshop window. Richard waited until he saw that he was alone. Then he hurried on down the street and he did not stop until he had reached the recruiting station and turned in at the gate.

It was on a fine summer day in 1777 when the new volunteer regiment left Hartford. It was on its long, weary way over rough roads to Peekskill on the Hudson, the headquarters of General Putnam. All Hartford was gathered on the wide porches and green streets to cheer the regiment on its way. All the children were there, too, waving their caps and bonnets.

All? No, one child was missing.

As the lines of blue swung along beneath the great old trees, the sound of a fife playing an old marching tune came piping above the shouting and the cheers of the crowd. Suddenly, everyone was quiet as the drummer came into sight and beside him a little lad of ten years, dressed in the uniform of the Colonies.

"Richard Jones!" the children whispered in excitement to each other. "It is our Richard, going to war with the regiment."

An old man leaning on his cane at the edge of the crowd took off his hat and called to Richard.

"Good-bye, little lad. If you play your fife as well as Grandfather taught you, it will put heart into the soldiers and strength in their arms. It was your fine piping that won you a place in the regiment, the youngest soldier of the Revolution. God save you and bring you back safe to us."

Hearing him, Richard stopped playing a moment and called out, "Good-bye, Grandfather. I'll try to do my duty. Good-bye!"

Then he was lost to sight—a little figure in a blue coat and knee breeches, Richard Lord Jones, enlisted at age ten in the army of the American Colonies.

Richard could play the fife better than anyone else in the regiment. It made the soldiers forget hunger and weariness and sleeplessness having the little lad march at their head—his merry tunes marking the time for their ragged shoes. He fifed the regiment all the long way to White Plains and then up the Hudson to Peekskill, where General Putnam was stationed and needed reinforcements. There he rested for a while, but not long. The British commander, General Clinton, appeared and captured two forts on the west side of the Hudson River. General Putnam was forced to retreat up the river.

It was a wild, adventure-filled retreat all the way. Richard had little but hard biscuit and raw salt pork to eat. He marched through villages that were in flames from the cannons of the British. He saw and was able to give information about a British spy, who was condemned and shot. Then the division to which Richard belonged reached Long Island, where it was commissioned to land at Huntington. The soldiers were in a common transport without guns, though, and it was captured by a British man-of-war. Richard, the little fifer, was marched with his colonel and the militia into the presence of a British commander.

The little lad must have looked very strange to the Englishman. His shoes were so worn that his feet were on the ground, and one could scarcely see the blue of his Continental uniform because of its dust and rags. He was pale from going without food and sleep, but he held his head very proudly and high. Not one of the prisoners was as brave as Richard as he marched into the presence of the enemy beside his colonel, carrying his fife under his arm.

"Who is this boy?" the British officer demanded, frowning down on the lad. His cabin was filled with swords and crowded with other officers of the king in scarlet broadcloth and gold lace. It was truly a fearful place for a little boy to be, but Richard answered bravely, "A soldier of the Colonies, sir."

The British officer laughed.

"What can a little boy like you do for the cause of these fighting farmers?" he asked. "I'll wager you're of no use and probably only a hindrance to your regiment."

Richard drew himself up proudly. "I have played the fife for the regiment these many months," he asserted boldly, "and they say there isn't a man in the army that can put as much heart into a tune as I. It might be that I could fight, too, if I was needed in battle."

A chorus of laughter from the British officers greeted Richard's last comment.

"You fight!"

"The little boy thinks he could fight!" they sneered, but the British commander looked sternly at Richard as he spoke to him.

"There is too much of this idle boasting in the farmer army. I want to put an end to it."

He motioned to an English lad, the boat captain's boy, older and more toughly built than Richard.

"Fight!" the officer commanded. "Let the Yankee fight one of King George's men!"

The two lads went at each other, rough and tumble. It was hardly a fair fight. The English lad hit right and left with iron fists, and Richard tried to block the blows, weak from his long marches and fasting. Richard's spirit and courage, however, were stronger than those of the other lad. First, one would be on top and then the other, while the British officers and Richard's own men shouted, "Down with the enemy of the king!" or "Down with King George!"

It was one of the strangest and most memorable fights of the whole War for Independence because both lads felt that more than their personal honor was at stake. Richard fell under his enemy's blows many times; but each time, he struggled to his feet, caught his breath, and struck back again.

"Enough!" the English lad finally cried out. And this battle, like so many others, was a victory for the Colonies.

There was little mercy shown by the British in those days, but one could not help but admire the courage of the youngest soldier of the regiment. The officer, whose prisoner he was, called Richard to him and patted him on his curly head.

"Truly, a brave little soldier!" he said. "As a reward for your good fighting, how would you like to have me give you your freedom?" he asked.

"Oh, sir," Richard cried, his whole face lighted with pleasure. "I should like it very much." But as he stepped closer to his own commander, he said, "I do not want to be released unless my colonel may come with me."

The British officer considered a moment. Then, in a sudden impulse of kindness, he granted Richard's request.

"Colonel Webb may go, too, on parole," he said.

Richard went home for a week in Hartford after his first fight. There had never been such a hero as he among the other boys and girls. He could not walk outside his gate without a crowd of them following at his heels, begging for stories from his adventures, a button, or a scrap of lining from his coat. The little soldier did not care for fame, though. He longed to be back in the thick of the fight, so he put his fife to his lips again and rejoined his regiment. They were glad to see him, for they had missed his cheerful tunes.

Richard was with the regiment when the famous Thaddeus Kosciusko, the great Polish freedom fighter, helped them fortify West Point, New York. Richard also marched over rough and frozen ground two hundred miles to Morristown, New Jersey; and, at the end of the weary way, General Washington greeted him. The winter of privation and exposure that followed was not so hard for Richard to bear, because he was sharing it with the great Washington. No other boy had so great an honor.

Through the three years of his enlistment, Richard faced whatever hardships came to him without a whimper, and the sound of his cheerful fife tunes comes down to us through all these years as one of the helps to America's freedom. He was honorably discharged from the Continental Army when he was a little more than thirteen years old. With an escort of two soldiers, he walked two hundred miles home.

No one asked him now what he could do for his country. Richard was the hero of the children and everyone else in Hartford. When the Revolution was over and the Stars and Stripes waved over the free Colonies, Richard knew that he had helped to win his country's independence.

Chapter 11

Betsy's Guest

Betsy looked with delight at the dainty white dress spread out on the big four-posted bed in the spare room.

It was early spring in the quaint old Southern town of Salisbury. Through the windows of the big white house of the Brandon plantation that was Betsy's home came the sweet notes of the first mockingbird, the singing of the farm hands as they plowed the land for the first planting, and the fresh odor of the pine trees.

A few years before, Salisbury had experienced the horrible destruction of war on its lovely green borders. Now, in the year of our Lord and of America's independence, 1791, the South was peacefully planting and harvesting once more. Barns and food cellars were full to overflowing.

The next day was to bring a great event to Salisbury, North Carolina. The President of the new United States, George Washington, and his cabinet were making a tour of the South. They had driven in lordly, lei-

108

surely fashion in their coaches through Virginia, South Carolina, and Georgia. All Salisbury would see the famous American in the morning.

The little town was ready for the President. He was to be met at the village green by an escort of soldiers who would accompany him as he toured the town, and flower girls were to head the parade.

Betsy Brandon was to be one of the flower girls, and that was why she had such a pretty new dress. It was made of the sheerest, white dotted cloth with as many pink ruffles as a rose has petals. Some of the ruffles

were caught up with bunches of tiny pink flowers and green leaves that Betsy's mother had made with her own hands. She also had a wide pink sash and a white hat with wide pink streamers and a bunch of the same pretty pink flowers in front. Betsy was to wear pink silk stockings and white slippers. Never, in all her life, had she been allowed to wear such lovely things.

She touched the flowing ruffles and the soft silk of the sash, thinking how happy she would be with the other little daughters of Salisbury in the morning. She had not noticed that her mother had entered the spare room and stood beside her looking down earnestly into the little girl's happy face. Mistress Brandon put her hand on Betsy's golden braids that hung neatly from the back of her head.

"My precious little daughter," Mistress Brandon said, "there is something that I must tell you."

"Yes, Mother," said Betsy, gazing into her mother's sober face.

Her mother spoke quickly now as though the words hurt her. "Your dear Aunt Tabitha's servant has just come in great haste on horseback from his mistress's plantation to say that she is sick and wishes me to come to her at once with a supply of medicines. I must go. The maids are packing my basket and laying out my traveling coat, and the horses are harnessed and at the door." She paused in sorrow at the grief that she saw suddenly in Betsy's radiant face.

"Your father will not return for some days yet," she added, and then stopped.

There was a pause and then Betsy looked up bravely, saying just what her mother had hoped and expected that she would, for she was a good little girl. "And Grandmother should not be left alone here because she is not well and the maids are new," Betsy said.

Then, all at once, it seemed as though she could not bear her disappointment. She threw herself into her mother's arms, burying her head in her shoulder. "I can't be a flower girl," she sobbed. "I must stay at home tomorrow and not see President Washington. Oh, I can't bear it; it seems as though I just can't!"

Her mother stooped down and kissed her. "Any other little daughter, except perhaps my own brave little Betsy, could not bear the disappointment," she said, "but she can. The Brandons come from a brave old family, strong to fight and well able to bear whatever comes to them. And think, too, dear, what sorrows came to our brave President before he won the war for us. You can try to be as brave as he, dear child, can you not?"

"Yes, Mother." Betsy was smiling again. She folded the dainty dress and the sash and laid them away in one of the lavender-scented drawers of the big mahogany cabinet. Then she went downstairs, and did not shed one tear as she kissed her mother good-bye and watched her drive away between the magnolia trees that lined the long driveway of the plantation.

It was a hard afternoon, though, for Betsy. The little girl who lived on the next plantation came over to see Betsy's dress and after she had shown it to her, Betsy

had to tell her that she would not have an opportunity to wear it. She thought, too, that it would make her grandmother feel bad if she were to know of her disappointment, so she sat with her in her big, sunny room in the afternoon and read to her and was a smiling little girl all the time. Late in the day, Betsy went down to the kitchen and made corn bread. She was almost as good a cook as was her mother. The corn bread was as yellow as gold and as light as sponge cake.

The morning of the great day for Salisbury was as blue and gold as sky and sun could make it. Betsy was up with the birds and gave the maids their orders for the day. She looked over the supplies in the safe, as the big locked food pantry was called, just as Mistress Brandon would have done if she had been home. She opened all the windows of the mansion to let in the sweet spring air. She filled the bowls and vases with fresh flowers, and then she sat down with her sewing on the porch.

Betsy was making a sampler in cross-stitch. Around the edge, embroidered in bright crewels, was a border of flowers and bees. Inside, Betsy was working her name in neat letters, the Lord's Prayer, and the date of her birth. Usually, Betsy liked nothing better than to be able to sit there in the quiet of the porch, the green lawn stretching below the steps and her colored sewing in her lap. Today, though, her eyes left her sewing project often to follow the line of the plantation driveway that led away from the house and down toward the village.

Through the trees she had glimpses of fluttering white skirts and bright ribbons. The flower girls, her little girl neighbors, were gathering and taking their happy way down to the village green to meet Mr. Washington. She could hear their merry voices and the sounds of fifes and drums. The soldiers were starting, too.

Betsy could see, in imagination, how pretty and joyful the town would be. People in their carriages and coaches would be there from miles around. Everyone would be joyous and so proud to do honor to the famous American. It was hours too early for him to be there yet, but here they were gathering to greet him.

"I am brave, but it seems as though I must cry just a little bit." Betsy buried her head in her sewing. But before she had shed a tear, a man's voice startled her. She looked up.

He was very tall and straight, and wore the beautiful, blue costume of the Colonies. His velvet knee breeches, silver-buckled shoes, gold-embroidered coat, and white wig showed Betsy that he was an important person. But he stood before her with his three-cornered hat in his hand and bowed to her as though she were a young lady.

"Good morning, little lass of Salisbury," he said in his deep, kind voice, pointing to her sewing. "You are a hard-working child, and I hope to see many children like you laboring in this new land. You work often in the day, and with the birds."

Betsy rose and dropped a deep curtsy to the stranger. She must have looked very winsome to him in her blue calico dress, white apron, and with her cheeks flushed to a rose color in excitement.

"My mother has taught me that work comes before play, and always in the morning," Betsy explained. "What is your pleasure, sir?" she went on. "I am the mistress of the Brandon plantation for the day. My mother is called away by the illness of my Aunt Tabitha and I am taking care of Grandmother and the maids in her absence. It is a sore disappointment to me, sir. I was to have been a flower girl in the village and to have walked with our guest of honor, Mr. Washington."

The stranger came up the steps, and took a chair beside Betsy.

"You wanted very much to see him?" he asked. "Why?"

"Because President Washington is a great soldier, and the most important man in the United States," Betsy answered, her hands folded and her eyes shining with excitement.

The man smiled. "I know him," he said. "Did it ever occur to you, little lass of Salisbury, that perhaps Mr. Washington is a lot like other Americans? He loves the earth," he pointed at the wide expanse of the fertile Brandon acres. "Perhaps, too, he likes to try new roads as I have done this morning. I have come a long distance," he said, "and am tired and hungry. I left my carriage at the entrance to your plantation, and the driveway looked so pleasant and quiet that I walked along it until I came to your house. May I ask you for food and drink, little Mistress of the Mansion?"

"Indeed yes, sir!" Betsy sprang toward the door; but, with her hand on the latch, she turned. "Do you like corn bread, sir?" she asked. "I made some, myself, yesterday afternoon. It is delicious with our fresh milk, half cream."

"That would make a breakfast that I should like above all else," the stranger said, smiling. He watched the graceful little figure as Betsy slipped through the door. "A good daughter of America," he said to himself, "a housewife above all else."

In the twinkling of an eye, Betsy returned, carrying a carefully spread tray. On the tray, there was placed gold and white china, thin and sparkling. The corn bread almost matched the gold, and a tall glass goblet was filled to the top with foamy milk. Betsy's guest ate as though no meal had ever tasted so good to him before. He did not speak until he had eaten the last

crumb of the corn bread and drunk the last drop of the milk. Then he rose to go.

"Many thanks, little Mistress of the Mansion," he said, "for your very gracious hospitality. I have been entertained most lavishly on the journey I am now taking, but at no stopping place have I enjoyed it so much. I want you to be comforted in your disappointment, my child, and to realize that in serving and feeding a stranger you have done as kind an act as if you had scattered flowers before your President."

"Thank you very much, sir!" Betsy bowed again, and took the strong hand the man gave her as he started down the steps. Then a sudden thought came to her. "May I ask your name, sir?" she asked. "I should like to tell my mother when she returns."

"You may, my child," he replied. "It is George Washington."

Comprehension Questions

1. In what year did this story take place?

2. What information was Betsy stitching on her cross-stitch sampler?

3. What food did Betsy give to her special guest?

4. Who was the person who came to visit Betsy?

5. Obeying your parents is not always easy. How did God choose to bless Betsy for her faithful spirit?

Chapter 12

The General and the Corporal

Here is a picture of the first President of the United States. Do I need to tell you his name? It is now over two hundred years since he died; but men will never grow tired of looking at his picture or of reading and talking about his deeds.

Why is this so? It is because he did so much to make this country the free, rich, happy land that it is.

If such a man as George Washington should walk the streets today, you would stop to look at him; everybody would stop and ask, "Who is he?" For his face, form, and manner would tell all who saw him that he was no common man.

George Washington was a tall man—more than six feet in height. He was well shaped and strong; his hands were very large, and his face was such as you see in the picture. It was he who led the armies of our country in the long war which gave us independence and made us a free people.

In times of danger there was no one more brave than he. In times of peace there was no one more wise than he. And in all the land there was no man to whom the people looked up with so much love and respect. And so it is truly said of him that he was "first in war, first in peace, and first in the hearts of his countrymen."

He was a great man, not only in great things, but in little things. He was never too great to do a kindness. He was never too high to stoop to those who were lower than he and in need of help. There was one rule which he tried always to obey. It was this: "Make sure you are doing what is right with God—then do it with all your strength."

One day, when his army was in camp, Washington walked out alone to enjoy the morning air and see what was happening. As it was winter, he had put on a long overcoat that hid his uniform; and so the soldiers among whom he passed did not know that he was the general.

At one place there was a young corporal with his men building a small fort made of logs. They were about to lift a very heavy log when Washington came up.

"Heave ho!" cried the little corporal. "Up with it, men! Up with it!" But he did not lift a hand to help his

men. The young men lifted with all their might. The log was almost in its place, but it was so heavy they could not move it any farther.

The corporal cried again, "Heave ho! Up with it!" The young soldiers could not lift it more; their strength was almost gone, and the log was about to fall.

Then Washington ran up, and with his strong arms gave them the help they so much needed. The big log was lifted upon the fort, and the men gave their thanks to the tall stranger who had been so kind. But the corporal said nothing.

"Why don't you take hold and help your men with this heavy lifting?" asked Washington.

"Why don't I?" said the little man. "Don't you see that I am the corporal?"

"Oh, indeed!" said Washington, as he unbuttoned his overcoat and showed the uniform which he wore. "Well, I am the general; and the next time you have a log too heavy for your men to lift, send for me."

You can imagine how the little corporal felt when he saw that it was General Washington who stood before him. It was a good lesson for him, and there are still little men living today who could learn a good lesson from this story. We find the source of this lesson in the Holy Bible, for it teaches that "He that will be chief among you, let him be your servant" (Matthew 20:27).

Comprehension Questions

1. What was the one rule George Washington always tried to obey?

2. The Bible teaches that "He that will be chief among you, let him be your servant." How did George Washington obey this verse?

3. What character in the story needed to learn this lesson?

4. Why did the soldiers not understand that the man who came to help them was the general?

Chapter 13

The Boy Who Guarded Washington

Levi and Asa Holden lived in Sudbury, in Massachusetts, before the War for Independence, but they had heard of old fights and of the courage of their ancestors.

On the shelf above their fireplace stood an ancient silver tankard—a contrast to the humble pewter and blue-and-white cups that flanked it. Graven on this silver tankard was a design of three pears in a cluster. This was the crest of the Holden family, and a reminder to the two boys of the battle in King Philip's War during which Grandfather Holden had held a road against the Indian warriors at the risk of his own life.

Asa was fourteen, and Levi a little older, when one morning there was a cloud of dust in the country road that lay in front of their farm, and a horseman dashed by calling at each door:

"The Redcoats have come! The British are on their way to Lexington! Take arms for the defense of the Colonies!"

So the farmers from miles around responded with the valor that makes history, and they marched toward Lexington and the bridge with their flintlock muskets. No boy or girl needs to be told how they held the bridge, how they went on to make their own history at Bunker Hill. But there is a part of the Battle of Lexington which is often untold.

When the smoke cleared away, and the sun shining on the weary farmers of Lexington showed them the Redcoats in retreat, two boys crawled from behind a haystack and began cleaning their muskets. Everyone stared in amazement at them. The Holden boys could shoot squirrels and an occasional deer, but no one knew that they had been with the volunteer regiment of farmers that had just saved the day for Colonial liberty.

But there they were, Asa and Levi Holden, two New England boys who had taken a part—and a brave part at that—in the memorable fight.

"I'm going on to Boston!" Levi told his brother. "I'm going to try to enlist in the Colonial Army even though I am not yet twenty. I look it, being so tall, and perhaps I can get a commission in the army. I want to be the Holden of my generation who held a road. But you mustn't come, Asa. You're only fourteen and you had best go home."

"All right, Levi," Asa said; but almost too readily, Levi thought. The farmer troops went on to Boston and so did Levi. Levi marched bravely with them, like the true Minute Man he was trying to be. There are old family papers telling how he acted as a lieutenant at the battle of Bunker Hill, leading a division of youths in their teens, as he still was.

And when Levi Holden was in the thick of the fight, who should he find behind the hay-walled heights of Bunker Hill but his brother Asa! Asa had trailed along at the end of the line, and Levi had the chance of saving his younger brother's life before the end of the affair.

After that, though, Asa had to go home. But Levi had so distinguished himself that he heard rumors among the officers of the Continental troops in regard to his promotion.

The great General Washington, who was being talked about as one of the coming men of the times, was stationed to the south in New Jersey. Levi was ordered to march south with a division, toward the commander of the army, and he had a high hope that he was going to be promoted.

Those first years of the revolution were full of unspeakable hardships. There were no good roads, no trains, no food, no proper clothing. Levi's shoes wore out before he reached Morristown, where General Washington was in headquarters, and his feet were torn and sore. There had been many encounters on the way, but through it all his heart was beating high with hope. Perhaps the commander would give him a horse. Surely he would at least be given a new sword!

So the ragged warriors came at last to Morristown, where the staff was quartered in tents and in log cabins. Lady Washington was there, her spinning wheel whirring industriously in the midst of the turmoil. And the great day came when young Levi Holden was called upon to stand before General Washington and receive his orders for the coming campaign.

Levi's courage shone out of his honest, brown eyes. His eagerness must have made the great commander a little sorry because of the duty that he had decided to assign to him.

"It is probable," Washington told Levi Holden, the boy who had carried a musket at Lexington and at Bunker Hill, "that during the course of the campaign my baggage, papers, and other matters of importance will have to be entrusted to someone. I am considering appointing you as lieutenant of my bodyguards, Holden. What say you to it?"

Levi gasped. That meant waiting on table, ordering the cook, keeping accounts, never getting into the thick of the fighting, but always being on guard at the doors and windows of staff headquarters. He had longed to feel a horse under him, to have the chance of waving a saber in the face of the enemy.

But as the boy considered, another thought came to him. In addition to General Washington's papers and baggage, of which he had just spoken, there was the unspoken trust of such a position as a lieutenant of the bodyguards, the trust of the commander's life. And Levi remembered also a passage from the Bible that he and Asa had been obliged to learn:

'A faithful man shall abound in blessings.'

"Thank you, General, for the appointment," Levi told Washington. "I will try to serve you and the staff well."

So Levi Holden did "kitchen police" work, as we would speak of it today, with all his soldierly might. How well the boy did it is told in one of the letters that General Washington wrote, and which has a bit of humor in it. He knew the trouble Levi had in helping him to give a dinner party in the mess tent. He knew when Levi took his place at the general's chair to pass the dishes, that there had been a struggle in the kitchen to keep up appearances of hospitality.

"I have asked some ladies to dinner," Washington wrote, "but am I not in honor bound to apprise them of their fare? It is needless to pretend that our table is large enough to hold the company. To say how it is usually covered is more essential, and this shall be the purpose of my letter.

"Since our arrival at this happy spot we have had a ham, sometimes a shoulder of bacon, to grace the table at the head. A piece of roast beef adorns the foot, and a dish of beans or greens, almost imperceptible, stands in the center.

"When the cook has a mind to set the table, which I presume will be the case tomorrow, we should have two beefsteak pies or dishes of crabs, one of each by the side of the center dish and dividing the space so that the distance from dish to dish is about six inches.

Without them it would be six feet, unless of course you count the decorations.

"Of late the cook has had the surprising intelligence to discover that apples will make pies, and it is hoped, in the violence of his efforts, we do not have a lumpy group of apple pies.

"If my guests can put up with such humble entertainment on plates, once tin but now iron, although not by virtue of scouring, I shall be happy to see them."

Among the guests whom Lieutenant Levi Holden helped Washington to entertain was Rochambeau, the French general who helped America in its War for Independence. The ladies came in their ruffles and laces, to be met by Lady Washington, who wore a homespun apron and was using her time in the knitting of a stocking.

"We must become independent," she told them gently, "by doing without those articles which we cannot make ourselves. While our husbands and brothers are examples of patriotism, we must be examples of industry."

And, helping to wait on the guests at this simple entertainment was the young lieutenant who wanted to fight but found his duty lying in a very different direction.

Levi was proud, though, when the weary, triumphant Colonials marched through Philadelphia, dusty and ragged, but with their general at the head of the line. Levi headed Washington's bodyguards with their flag, a figure in the uniform of the guard holding a horse by the bridle and, beside it, Liberty leaning on the shield of the union, which was supported by an eagle.

The guards looked very well in their uniforms—blue coats faced with buff, red waistcoats, white body belts, black halfgaiters and black felt hats bound with white tape. Also, their banner was made of white silk, on which the emblems were sewed in colors.

Soon Levi went home to Sudbury again. He brought trophies to lay on the shelf above the fireplace beside his grandfather's silver one. No decoration for valor in battle, not a scalp, not a broken sword, not his musket. No, indeed, none of these.

Levi placed there a handspun and hand-woven nightcap, very snug and comfortable, which Lady Washington had made to keep him warm when he stood all night at guard at her doorstep. And, beside it, Levi laid the last bill for kitchen supplies, neatly approved and signed by General Washington.

Levi Holden had stood and waited on his commander during the revolution, but he held in his heart the pride of knowing that he had helped make the union possible, and the life of its first President secure.

Comprehension Questions

1. What war did Levi Holden's grandfather fight in?

2. In what battle did Levi act like a lieutenant, leading the division of youths in their teens?

3. Levi hoped to be promoted by General Washington, but was appointed lieutenant of Washington's body-guards instead. What Bible verse encouraged the disappointed boy soldier?

4. Describe some of Levi's duties.

5. What was the trophy Levi brought home to lay on the shelf above the fireplace beside his grandfather's silver one?

Chapter 14

Visiting at Mount Vernon

Any boy or girl would have loved the great farm at Mount Vernon, where George Washington went to live after serving as the first President of the United States. In fact, it was not one farm but several; like a small village, of which the big white house—with its tall pillars, huge kitchen, and many fireplaces—was the center.

It lay on the right bank of the Potomac River, with Mr. Washington's own wharf, from which he shipped tobacco, flour, and many barrels of shad and herring to England. He raised the wheat in his own fields and ground it into flour at his own mill, and every barrel of it was stamped: "George Washington, Mount Vernon." That meant that it did not have to be opened by the men at the customs house, for everyone knew what good flour was ground in Washington's mill.

If you could have paid a visit to Mount Vernon— long, long ago, in the year 1799—you would have

started from the wharf and taken a walk to the different parts of the estate of Mount Vernon, each interesting in its own way.

There was the River Farm, with its tobacco fields lying along the bank of the river. There was Dogue-Run Farm and Muddy-Hole Farm and Union Farm, named after our country gained its independence, and the Mansion-House Farm. There were ducks and roosters and chickens and mules and cows and pigs and horses; all the four-footed friends that you love, and which Mr. Washington also loved.

Martha Washington, at this time, had a very clever kind of a hole cut in the wall of their house so that the favorite cat could come in on a cold night. It was hung from a hinge at the top, and old letters say that this cat-hole opened right into Martha Washington's own room.

Your walk around the grounds of Mount Vernon would have taken you through the most delightful woods, for George Washington loved trees, and believed

that they should form part of a nation's wealth. He did all that he could to preserve his woodland. A letter that he wrote to one of his farm superintendents at Mount Vernon, from Philadelphia, tells us this:

"It is much to be regretted," wrote President Washington, "and I do regret it exceedingly, that the honey locusts which have been set out should have perished. It would seem as if I never would get forward in my plan of hedging.

"With respect to the transplanting of cedar, or any other evergreen, I am persuaded there is no other sure way of getting them to live than by taking them up in the winter with a block of frozen earth around the roots, and as large as can conveniently be obtained. This not only gives them their mother earth, but by its adhesion to the roots, it nourishes the body until the fibers from the former grow sufficiently to secure the thriftiness of the plant.

"I transplanted thousands of pine and cedar trees, getting scarcely any to live until I adopted the above method; after which, so long as it was practiced, I never lost one. Witness the pine groves by the gardens!"

Also, we may read in Washington's diary dated March 21, 1763, of a busy day spent in his fruit orchards.

"Grafted 40 cherry trees as follows: 12 Bullock Hearts, a large black May cherry; 18 very fine May cherry and 10 Coronation. Also grafted 12 Magnum Bonum plums. Also planted 4 nuts of the Mediterranean Palm in the pen where the chestnut grows. Set out 55 cuttings of the Madeira grape, and planted twenty Spanish pears."

Following the paths and trails of Mount Vernon, you would look in through the doorway of a pleasant schoolhouse where the children of the Washington servants and farmhands were taught. As you travel, you might chance upon a big barn known as the neighborhood corn-house, which was filled, through George Washington's orders, with corn every year. This was for the sole use of the poor of the neighborhood, particularly the women and children, that they might be saved from starvation. Mr. Washington did this because he knew that the Holy Bible directs farmers to make their surplus crops available to poor widows and orphans.

He also owned several fishing stations on the Potomac, at which excellent herring were caught. And herring, when salted, were an important article of food for the poor.

For the good and help of his neighborhood, the master of Mount Vernon set aside one of these fishing stations on one of the best of all his docks, and furnished it with poles and nets and drying frames. Here the poor of the surrounding countryside might fish free, at any time, by only an application to an overseer. And if a small boy made such a large haul that he had difficulty getting it to shore, by Washington's orders, this young fisherman was given help with his net.

Everything about the farm was shipshape, and the best tools to be had at this time were provided. You may listen to Washington himself as he tells farmers of today how he felt about his business of agriculture. He wrote this in a letter to one of his Mount Vernon superintendents:

"I am never sparing, with proper economy, in furnishing my farms with any and every kind of tool and implement that is calculated to do good and neat work. I not only authorize you to buy the kind of plows you were speaking to me about, but any other tools the utility of which you have proved from your own experience; particularly a kind of hand rake which Mr. Stuart tells me is used on the eastern shore of Maryland, instead of hoes, for corn at a certain stage of its growth.

"In short, I shall begrudge no reasonable expense that will contribute to the improvement and neatness of my farms for nothing pleases me better than to see them in good order, and everything trim, handsome, and thriving. While nothing hurts me more than to find them otherwise, the tools and implements lying wherever last used, exposed to injury from rain and sun."

When you had finished your walk over the estate and returned to the Mansion-House Farm, you would have crossed the threshold and gone into the library of the house. You would have stepped softly, for an old gentleman with a powdered wig sat, wrapped in blankets, by the window. He was writing, in the winter sunshine, a letter to a man of whom he was very fond and in whom he placed a great deal of trust. This man was James Anderson, a Scotsman who was the superintendent of the Mount Vernon farms.

Mr. Washington would surely have let you read the pages of his letter to his farmer, as he finished each and carefully dusted it with his sand sifter—as you know, dusting helps dry the ink. His heart was full of concern for his animals out in the barns that winter, and he was writing instructions about what he wanted done to keep them comfortable. Washington also wrote advice to Mr. Dobbin, his faithful farm worker.

"The work-horses and mules must always be in their stalls when it is cold, and the stalls all littered and cleaned," he instructed his farmer, "and they are to be plenteously fed with cut straw and as much chopped grain, meal, and bran, with a little salt mixed there-with, as will keep them in good condition for work. See, also, that they are watered as often as they are fed. This as concerns their winter food.

"For spring, summer, and autumn, it is expected that feeding them on green food—first with rye and next with clover, with only a little grain—will enable them to perform their work.

"The stables and farm pens ought to be kept well bedded and the stalls very clean for the comfort of my animals. As straw cannot be afforded for the litters, leaves and weeds should be gathered for the stables, and leaves and cornstalks for the pens and the sheep runs.

"In like manner let the people, with their blankets, go every evening to the nearest woods to fill them with leaves, bottoming the animals' beds with cornstalks and then covering them thick with leaves. This will save food and make the beasts lie warm and comfort-able."

Next there was a neatly written page to Mr. Anderson about the "Friendly Cow." There was never a lack of

rich milk and clotted cream on George Washington's farms, and this was because he was good to his cattle.

"The oxen and other horned cattle," he wrote, "are to be housed from the first of November until the first of May, and they are to be fed as well as the means of the farm will admit. The oxen must always be kept in good condition in their stalls and the cows, so many of them as can find places, in the barns. The rest, with the other cattle, must be put in newly erected sheds, and all carefully watered every day."

So this kind old gentleman wrote on. The pigs must be well fed and kept clean. The farm tools must be oiled and polished. One field that had been overworked with several crops should be allowed to rest for a year. Some of the apple trees and the berry bushes would need trimming later.

There was not a single instruction put down that a boy or girl could not understand and help in carrying out. Much as you would have wished for the writing to go on, it stopped at last, and the orders were sent to the farmer.

Mr. Washington leaned back among his blankets, not feeling very well that winter, and looked out over the white fields of Mount Vernon. He was not thinking of the Revolution, or the Declaration of Independence, or about anything of national importance. He wanted to be sure that his barn friends were kept comfortable when he was not able to go out on his horse, and ride the length of the farms, to inspect them.

If you ever have the opportunity to water a horse or gather some leaves and cornstalks to make a bed for a patient cow, just remember that this is what George Washington would like you to do.

The noble spirit of George Washington can be seen in the way he showed concern and compassion for common animals. No person should ever think that he can become so high and mighty that his obligation to show kindness to God's creatures is no longer necessary.